Don't Cry
Past Tuesday

Don't Cry Past Tuesday

Hopeful Words for Difficult Days

2nd Edition

Charles E. Poole

Foreword by Charles B. Bugg

SMYTH&HELWYS

PUBLISHING, INCORPORATED • MACON, GEORGIA

Smyth & Helwys Publishing, Inc.
6316 Peake Road
Macon, Georgia 31210-3960
1-800-747-3016
©1991, 1996, 2000 by Smyth & Helwys Publishing
All rights reserved.
First Edition, 1991
Second Edition, 2000
Printed in the United States of America.

Charles E. Poole

The paper used in this publication meets the minimum requirements of
American National Standard for Information Sciences—Permanence of
Paper for Printed Library Materials.
ANSI Z39.48–1984. (alk. paper)

Library of Congress Cataloging-in-Publication Data

Poole, Charles E.
    Don't cry past Tuesday: hopeful words for difficult days /
    Charles E. Poole; foreword by Charles B. Bugg
    ISBN 1-57312-319-6
    pp.   cm.
    1. Sermons, America.
    2. Southern Baptist Convention—Sermons.
    3. Baptists—Sermons.
    I. Title. II. Title: Don't cry past Tuesday.
    BX6333.P675D86   2000
    252'.06132—dc20   CIP
                                            91-42264

To Marcia
bearer of grace, keeper of hope

Contents

Preface to the Second Edition

Tucked away in Alfred Tennyson's poem "In Memoriam" is that wonderful verse on the limits of words in the face of grief:

> I sometimes hold it half a sin
> To put in words the grief I feel
> For words, like Nature, half reveal
> And half conceal the soul within.

Anyone who has ever staggered through deep darkness and great grief knows the truth of Tennyson's lament. When it comes to life's most complex problems and devastating losses, there is a place where words cannot go. Our words conceal as much as they reveal. And yet, I have long known that my calling in life is to say and write words that speak to those who grieve and struggle and wonder about God. It is out of that passion that *Don't Cry Past Tuesday* emerged ten years ago.

This second edition of *Don't Cry Past Tuesday* contains only a few minor changes from the original edition, but I am grateful to those who guide the life of Smyth and Helwys Publishing for allowing me to work back through these pages and remove the pronouns for God. In the decade since I wrote the words in *Don't Cry Past Tuesday* I have ceased using pronouns for God. God is not He or Him. Neither is God She nor Her. "He" and "She" are human categories that denote gender. God is not a male or a female. God is God. Thus, I have come to believe that it is best to avoid, when possible, using any pronoun for God. I am thankful that this new edition of *Don't Cry Past Tuesday* more nearly reflects that conviction.

In the years since this book first took shape, I have lost my dear father, Olif Hubert Poole, to cancer. Marcia, Joshua, Maria, and I have said goodbye to family and friends because we moved and death came. Thus, there has been more grieving than I knew when the words that follow were written. But we have learned better what we knew a little; that God enables us to live through things that, if someone had told us we were going to have to face, we would not have believed we could bear. We all do a good bit of weeping along the way, but we "don't cry past Tuesday," because, by the grace of God, we live through things, life moves on, and we live to laugh again, to rest again, to actually rejoice and be glad again. Thanks be to God.

Charles E. Poole
Jackson, Mississippi
Easter 2000

Foreword

S everal years ago I met a young minister for whom I felt instant affection. It was not just that we shared the same first name and suffered the indignities that go with unusual last names. Rather, Chuck Poole was a person of unusual gifts and extraordinary sensitivity.

My appreciation for him has grown even more as I have come to know more of the depth out of which he ministers to people. When I preached a revival in his church, I felt the genuine love that the people at First Baptist, Macon, have for their pastor. Their affection for Chuck grows out of their gratitude not only for his pastoral gifts but also for the warm, sensitive person that he is.

Readers of these sermons will quickly discover that warmth and sensitivity. Chuck Poole does what an effective preacher must do. First he turns to the biblical text and exegetes it with care and insight, but Chuck also turns to people and "exegetes" us with understanding and compassion. Then he weds the Word of God to our lives in a way that deepens our faith and makes us even more thankful for the "God of Grace and God of Glory."

I am pleased that Chuck Poole will enlarge his ministry with this book of sermons. This pastor/preacher has already enriched the lives of many, and I predict that in the days ahead, he will encourage the lives of many more.

The sermons in *Don't Cry Past Tuesday* have blessed me and given me a stronger hope as I have read them. They will do the same for you. I am grateful for my friend, Chuck Poole, whose preaching really makes a difference and through whom we hear clearly about the God of Christ who makes all the difference.

Charles B. Bugg
Pastor, Providence Baptist Church
Charlotte, North Carolina

Acknowledgments

When you owe so much to so many, acknowledgment becomes a rather unnerving task. To echo the apostle loosely, "I am in debt to most everybody out there!"

I am a grateful debtor to my teachers, chief among them such giant souls as Howard Giddens of Mercer University, and Chevis Horne and John Carlton of the old Southeastern Baptist Theological Seminary. To them I owe a debt that shall never be fully paid.

I am thankful for the "far-off" influence of Fred Craddock, L. D. Johnson, Carlyle Marney, Henri Nouwen, Frederick Buechner, and John Claypool. Their books have shaped my life, colored my eyes, and lifted my sight.

Charles Bugg and Kirby Godsey have honored my stammerings by bracketing this book with the front and back parentheses of their kind words. I thank them for their encouragement and friendship.

The good people of Smyth & Helwys Publishing Company have brought these words to the light of day with patient attention and diligent effort. To them I am grateful, as well as to church secretary Pattie Brown who typed this work from my often chaotic pen and ink.

Near the last, I must declare my great debt to the grand old church at the top of the Polar. The First Baptist Church of Macon,

Georgia is the family of faith in which I have learned best the lessons of grace and hope. I acknowledge with gratitude the affirmation, patience, and acceptance with which these words have been received by the people of God who stumble up the steps of that great old church.

At last, I acknowledge that I would have little to say or write without the grace gifts of love and laughter that have come to me from Marcia, Joshua, and Maria. They bear the grace, keep the hope, and live the life.

Chuck Poole
Pentecost 1991
At the Top of Poplar

On Preaching
in the Cry Room

A bumpy slice of old brick street winds around the front of our sanctuary at the top of Poplar in Macon. That old relic of a road ought to have a pretty good case of religion, what with First Baptist Church bumping into its curb on one side, and St. Joseph's Catholic Church looking down over its other shoulder.

I walked over to Saint Joseph's one day to borrow a book from my friend, Father Cuddy. As I made my way across the old brick street and toward the great cathedral, I caught sight of an intriguing little sign that was stationed near a sanctuary entrance. It was a simple metal sign; black, with two words painted in white. "CRY ROOM," said the sign. That's all. Just two words on the little sign near the huge sanctuary: CRY ROOM.

I later learned that "cry room" is another name for nursery. The cry room sign points young families to a small room in which parents can hold their babies while viewing the mass. In the cry room, babies can cry and make other baby-type noises without being heard by the rest of the congregation. The cry room is made for crying!

I often think about that sign, standing at a sanctuary door, pointing the way to a room where it's alright to cry. I have about decided that maybe there ought to be a little sign that says CRY ROOM standing out front at every sanctuary of every church everywhere. And it ought to point, not to a side room for little people, but to the main room for big people.

After all, big people need a cry room most of all. Big people need a cry room: a place to confess their deepest guilt, ask their toughest questions, and tell their darkest stories. Big people need a cry room: a place where they can find help with all the heavy luggage of their unhealed diseases, their unrealized ambitions, their unresolved mysteries, and their unfulfilled hopes. Big people need a cry room.

Maybe there ought to be a little sign that says CRY ROOM keeping vigil outside the door of every sanctuary everywhere. The sanctuary of the church must always and ever be a cry room for big people . . . a place where the shoulder-stooping, sleep-robbing, heartbreaking fears, shames, and hurts of life are voiced, not silenced; acknowledged, not denied. The sanctuary of the church must always and ever be a cry room for big people . . . a place where the protest of hope is lodged against the evidence for despair. The sanctuary of the church must always and ever be a cry room for big people . . . where folks who limp through the narthex, bludgeoned by the hard twists and turns of life, can rest up, heal up, and hear—all over again—the gospel of grace and hope.

Here is where the preacher comes in. The preacher's chance, when the hour strikes, is the chance to say a word of hope and grace to the crowd that limped out of the world, up the steps, through the doors, and into the cry room.

No one has so nearly captured the possibilities of a preacher in a cry room as has Frederick Buechner in that oft-quoted passage from his wonderful book *Telling the Truth*:

> So the sermon hymn comes to a close with a somewhat unsteady amen, and the organist gestures the choir to sit down . . . The preacher pulls the little cord that turns on the lectern light and deals out his note cards like a riverboat gambler. The stakes have never been higher. Two minutes from now he may have lost his listeners completely to their own thoughts, but at this minute he has them in the palm of his hand. The silence in the shabby church is deafening . . . Everybody knows the kind of things [the preacher]

has told them before and not told them, but who knows what this time, out of the silence [the preacher] will tell them? Let [the preacher] tell them the truth.[1]

Buechner is right. So much is at stake. The preacher does have a real chance to make a real difference, but only if he or she dares to tell the truth. The preacher does have a real chance to make a real difference, but only if she or he is willing to say real words of real hope to the real pain of the real world.

Needless to say, the sermon is not the only act of worship in which the hope and grace of the gospel are offered and received. The hymns and anthems, the organ and offering, the prayers and silences, the scripture lessons and handshakes, and laughter and tears, and even (or especially!) the rest and stillness . . . all of these are means of grace and structures of hope that enable us to rest up and heal up in the cry room where we keep going back by, Sunday after Sunday.

The sermon is not everything, nor is it the only thing. But surely it can be, should be, must be, something in the drama of corporate worship. At its best, the sermon is something, something that lodges a protest of hope against all the evidence for despair. At its best, the sermon is a protest of hope that wedges the gospel of grace between us and our anxiety, guilt, and pain. That is the primary hope with which these sermons are offered: the hope that these words will become bearers of grace to the troubled and keepers of hope for the weary.

Like all sermons, they are not what they should have been. I keep a little cassette tape in the top left drawer of my study desk. It is a tape of a Sunday morning sermon. It was mailed to someone who had called in a request for it. The recipient sent it back with a little piece of paper taped across the top of the cassette. The paper said "Defective and Incomplete."

The note did not indicate whether it was the tape or the sermon on the tape that was defective and incomplete! I saved it as an unintentional, serendipitous reminder that all sermons are both defective *and* incomplete. The sermons that follow certainly merit both adjectives. But, though defective and incomplete, they do seek to bear grace and speak hope. They are offered with the prayer that the weary, lonely, sad, and frightened will be able to find the hope of the gospel tucked away in some waiting corner of some stammered sermon.

There are, frankly, a couple of secondary and parenthetical ambitions tagging along with that primary purpose. They are minor homiletical hopes. They are tangential "preacher" concerns, along for the ride.

One of those secondary ambitions is to demonstrate the premise that preaching can be thoroughly biblical without necessarily being "expository" or even strictly textual or obviously exegetical. Expository and exegetical approaches to preaching are certainly useful and important, but they do not constitute the only paths that lead to the "biblical" pulpit. A sermon that is true to the spirit of Christ, the gospel of God, and the witness of scripture is biblical, with or without the exegesis of the text or the exposition of verse after verse. (There are many examples of this understanding of biblical preaching, but more of them, I suspect, are to be found outside my own denomination than within it.)

Needless to say, a person can preach biblically with a text and unbiblically without one, but, as James Cox has so well said, a person can preach biblically without a text and unbiblically with one![2] Verse by verse exposition does not automatically guarantee a biblical sermon, and the absence of exposition does not automatically presuppose an unbiblical sermon. The most "biblical" sermon is that sermon that is most true to the spirit of Christ and the gospel of grace and hope.

Fred Craddock's wisdom is immensely helpful at this point. Writing about the sermon and the scripture, Professor Craddock says,

> It is possible that a sermon that buries itself in the text, moves through it phrase by phrase, and never comes up for air may prove to be "unbiblical" in the sense that it fails to achieve what the text

achieves. On the other hand, a sermon may appear to be walking alongside rather than through a text, or may seem to pause, now and then to look up at the lofty peak of a text so extraordinary as to defy the skills of the most experienced preacher, and yet be quite "biblical" in the sense of releasing that text to do its work among the listeners.[3]

All this in no way reduces the place of scripture in the church and the pulpit, nor is this an invitation into the lavender fog of rootless, personal, subjective opinion. Indeed, to quote again from Fred Craddock:

> The scriptures are normative in the life of the church. To sever preaching from that norm either by neglect or intent would be to cut the church off from its primary source of nourishment and discipline. Sermons not informed and inspired by Scripture are objects dislodged, orphans in the world, without father or mother.[4]

The sermons that follow are, in no case, expository. Some of them are not, strictly speaking, textual, but all of them are offered under the authority and in the spirit of the sacred scriptures. Perhaps they will serve as additional witnesses to the many valid "forms" of "biblical" preaching.

The other secondary, and homiletical, concern is my conviction that the pastoral preaching of hope is shaped by the life of pastoral care. The pastoral sermon of hope requires the discipline of study, prayer, and reflection, but it also requires the life of pastoral care. The pastoral preaching of hope is made authentic by a life spent "getting under" the loads of pain, bewilderment, and struggle that our sisters and brothers must bear.

In this sense, the enormous pastoral care demands that tug at the parish preacher constitute no rival to the pulpit. (The real rival to the pulpit is church administration, that many-tentacled monster that leaves us, as Carlyle Marney once said, "stoned to death with popcorn"!) The life of pastoral care, though it is often exhausting and frequently depleting, is no rival to the work of pastoral preaching.

Indeed, it is in the empathetic life of pastoral care that authentic pastoral preaching is born.

Such talk as this is easy grist for the mill of misunderstanding! All of this is not to say that we haunt the halls of human suffering "looking for a sermon." No. It is just that in the sacrament of "weeping with those who weep and rejoicing with those who rejoice" we are changed. We become sensitive and soft-spoken. We are transformed by what Wayne Oates called the revelation of God in human suffering.

In the presence of human suffering, our humanity is baptized in the deep and mysterious waters of our last and only hope, the hope of the resurrection. And at the same time, in the presence of human suffering, our baptism is humanized by the swift and rushing waters of life's hardest twists and turns. Out of the sacrament of shared pain our humanity is baptized, our baptism is humanized, and we are enabled to speak with both passion and compassion of our common trials in the world and our common hope in the resurrection.

(Parenthetically, this, of course, may not be for everyone. Native temperament is a factor in ministry. Some personality types are geared to big programs, budget promotions, and growth strategies—all of which are important. Other personality types are tilted toward moving slowly and silently through this world, entering into the pain and joy, anxiety and despair of those around them. I suppose some ministers can be both ways; I am not sure.)

Suffice it to say that a study with books is indispensable to prepare a pastoral sermon, but a world with people is indispensable to prepare a pastoral preacher. Pastoral preachers might best be distinguished by the image of a bad bruise and the gait of a slow limp than by the image of a glowing success and the gait of a powerful stride. The pastoral preaching of hope is authenticated, shaped, and nurtured by the life of pastoral care. But enough of this "preacher talk."

Those homiletical concerns are subordinate to the one larger hope that these sermons will help the hurting. We will not likely find a more magnificent statement of the preacher's only worthy ambition than that arresting paragraph from Joseph Sittler's *Gravity and Grace:*

> That's what a sermon is for: to hang the holy possible in front of the mind of the listeners and lead them to that wonderful moment when they say, "If it were true, it would do." To pass from that to belief is the work of the Holy Spirit, not of the preacher or the teacher.[5]

That is the preacher's greatest possibility: to so honestly and faithfully confess the outlandish hope of the gospel that the listeners are led to that wonderful moment when they say "if it were true, it would do."

A sermon, defective and incomplete though it may be, is worth the enormous investment it demands if God uses it to "hang the holy possible in front of the listeners." That is the ambition of these homilies.

Specifically, there are three sermons that seek to "hang the holy possible" in front of the minds of those who struggle with death, loss, and grief: "The Strange Gift of Grief," "Don't Cry Past Tuesday," and "After Easter: What Is Death for Those Who Live?"

There are three sermons that seek to "hang the holy possible" in front of the minds of those who bear seemingly endless burdens: "How Long?" "The Porch Is Never Empty," and "The Things I Cannot Change."

There are four sermons that seek to "hang the holy possible" in front of the minds of those who are frightened and bewildered by the sheer difficulty of life: "Hard Things Are Hard," "No More Sea," "The Last Word Is Hope," and "If They Only Knew."

Finally, there are two sermons that seek to "hang the holy possible" in front of the minds of those who wonder if they have anything at all to offer God or anybody else: "I Saw Your Face, and It Looked Like God" and "If You Wait until You're Strong."

These sermons are like all sermons: they are "defective and incomplete." But they are sent forth with the prayer that they might hang the holy possible out there where we can see it and lead us to that wonderful moment when we say of the hope of the gospel: "If that is true, it is enough! If that is true, it will do!"

A few years ago, a minister friend asked me if I had any idea why our church receives such a large number of appeals for help from persons who are in need of food and clothing. He had heard about the frequency of our church's conversations with, and ministry to, "transient" persons. He wanted to know why so many hungry, troubled souls seem to find their way to the old First Church.

I responded with the usual answers about being a downtown church and about the large numbers of homeless persons. Then, quite without thinking, I wrapped up that "off the cuff" reply with an even "offer the cuff" speculation. "You know," I observed, "lots of unemployed people travel the interstate highways in search of work and in need of help. Our church sits on a high, high hill, and you can see the huge twin towers of the sanctuary from the Spring Street exit off I-16. So, I guess some of them just come to the steeples."

It wasn't a brilliant answer. It may not have been an accurate sociological assessment. But ever since I've been thinking about the way people come to the steeples and what they long to find beneath the steeples in the house of God.

Sometimes, people come *hungry* to the steeples.
Sometimes, people come *homeless* to the steeples.
Sometimes, people come *happy* to the steeples.
Sometimes, people come *nonchalantly* to the steeples.
Sometimes, people come *routinely* to the steeples.
Sometimes, people come *limping* to the steeples.
Sometimes, people come *skipping* to the steeples.
Sometimes, people come *lonely* to the steeples.
Sometimes, people come *angry* to the steeples.
Sometimes, people come *depressed* to the steeples.
Sometimes, people come *bewildered* to the steeples.
Sometimes, people come *weary* to the steeples.
Sometimes, people come *disappointed* to the steeples.

People come to the steeples because they assume that wherever there is a steeple at the top there is a sanctuary at the bottom. People come to the steeples to find beneath the spires a cry room where fears can be voiced, sins can be confessed, tears can fall, questions can rise, and grace can accept. People come to the steeples hoping against hope that there will be a real sanctuary beneath the steeples. People come to the steeples to rest up, heal up, and start out again, nourished by the rituals they keep, the people they see, the hymns they sing, the prayers they raise, and the sermon they hear.

We come to the steeples yearning for a sanctuary, looking for a big people cry room and listening for the enduring hope of the gospel. We come to the steeples, holding in our hands all the fears that hold us back. We come to the steeples, dragging behind us all the regret that drags us down. We come to the steeples, pulling in our wake all the fatigue that pulls us under.

Beneath the steeples there is a cry room. Inside the cry room there is a pulpit. Behind the pulpit there is a preacher. Let the preacher stand beneath the steeples and announce the gospel of grace and hope to all who come to the cry room.

Notes

[1]Frederick Buechner, *Telling the Truth* (San Francisco: Harper & Row, 1977) 22-23.

[2]James Cox, *A Guide to Biblical Preaching* (Nashville: Abingdon, 1976) 24.

[3]Fred Craddock, *Preaching* (Nashville: Abingdon, 1985) 28.

[4]Ibid., 27.

[5]Joseph Sittler, *Gravity and Grace* (Minneapolis: Augsburg, 1986) 63.

Chapter 1

No More Sea

Revelation 21:1-4

I t is not likely that we will soon again see the likes of Carlyle Marney. He has been gone from us for more than a decade now, but we continue to find rest in the lingering shadow of his enormous witness.

In 1963, Marney wrote a book called *Recovery of the Person.* He included in that book a description of "the heaven of his fancy." He followed the pattern of our scripture lesson and listed lots of things that would need to be absent from heaven. Here are some of the things Marney hoped not to find inside the gates:

> The heaven of my fancy would contain no Democrats, no Republicans . . . no games, no puzzles, no charts, no calendars, no engagements pads . . . no germs, no debts, no money . . . no brussel sprouts, no elections . . . no professional pastors . . . no finance campaigns . . . no experts on anything . . . no pills, tranquilizers, hair curlers, tweezers, or stiff petticoats . . . and no Saturday evenings without a sermon ready.[1]

That was Marney's list of what would not be in heaven if he were in charge. You could make your own list, and so could I. But the list that matters most has already been made. It is a wonderful recital of the things that will not bother us when we enter the unhindered, uninterrupted presence of God. It is the "no more" catalog that is tucked away in the last book of the Bible.

Let us run through that list one more time: no more death, no more sorrow, no more crying, no more pain, no more sea. That is a mighty fine list, but something in there does not quite seem to belong. In the catalog of things that will not be, one thing seems slightly out of place. In the presence of God, there will be no more death, no more sorrow, no more crying, and no more pain. So far so good. But there is one thing on John's list that does not quite seem to fit. It is, in fact, the very first thing that John says will not be: "And I saw a new heaven and a new earth, and there was no more sea." No more sea. No more sea?

What in the world can he mean: no more sea? How does "no more sea" fit in with "no more death, no more sorrow, no more pain, no more crying?" I mean, after all, we like the sea. The sea is where the beach is, and the beach is where the shrimp are! Why, just last summer, "me and mine" were strolling along the edge of the sea, listening to the rhythm of the waves. I speculated to Marcia that quietly walking on the fringe of the ocean was probably the way the Lord really intended for life to be lived. And then, lo and behold, I read in the last book of the Bible that there will be "no more sea" when we get to heaven.

No more sea? What can that mean? Why would the catalog of troubles that will someday no longer plague the people of God begin with the sea? What was John trying to say? What did he hope to tell his audience with that strange announcement, "No more sea"?

When John said that one day there would be "no more sea," his congregation did not find his sentence strange. They found it wonderful. "No more sea" did not sound out of place to their ears. "No more sea" sounded just fine to the folks who first read that trio of words.

"The sea" had acquired a bad reputation with the original audience of this Revelation. The sea had written a long resume with those souls who opened this letter and read it before we did. Their sons and husbands had gone to sea and never returned. Their grandparents had told their strange tales of great monsters that made havoc of boats and people. They had not learned to cope with the sea's waves or control the sea's power or conquer the sea's depths. The sea was too strange. The sea was too big. The sea was too dangerous.

The sea was pregnant with unlimited possibilities for evil. And not only that, the sea was the non-negotiable barrier that separated John, the island exile, from the people to whom he wrote. It was the sea that separated people from their loved ones. The sea dared the brave. The sea devoured the daring. The sea defied passage. The sea was a heaving, seething, canyon that yawned its jaws to swallow the good and engulf the strong. The sea was something to dread. The sea was something to hate. The sea was something to fear. For John on the island and his friends on the mainland, the sea was simply the scariest thing in the world.

So, when John started out his recital of "the notable absences in the presence of God,"[2] "no more sea" was anything but out of place. In fact, without "no more sea," the list, for those folks, would have been woefully incomplete. They did not want any more sea. "The sea" to them meant dread. "The sea" to them meant anxiety. "The sea" to them meant fear. "No more sea" meant no more anything to be afraid of. "No more sea" meant that, one of these days, in the presence of God, there will be nothing left to fear. "No more sea" meant that somehow, somewhere, someday, some way, there would be no reason for anybody to be afraid.

"No more sea" sounded just fine to John's congregation, because to him and them it meant that one day there will not be anything left to fear. And if "no more sea" means nothing left to dread and no more reason to be scared, then "no more sea" sounds just fine to you and me. After all, most every one of us is scared of something. (The only people who do not admit that they are afraid are those who are afraid they will seem weak if they admit that they are afraid!) Most of our fear is not the frantic fright of stampeding panic. Most of our fear is more like the vague uneasiness of creeping anxiety. Some of our fears are paranoid imaginations. Some of our fears are of threats very real. But all of us are acquainted with what John called "the sea." We know what it is to be scared.

One of these days, there will be no more sea, no more anything to be afraid of, no more reason to be scared. No more sea means no more anything to fear. But until the day when there is no more sea, there is much more sea. Until the day finally comes when there will be no more fears, there are plenty of fears. So . . . Which one is yours? Name your sea! What is your greatest fear? What scares you? Of what are you most afraid? Go ahead . . . name your sea.

For some of us, the name of the sea is sickness. The most frightening words in the world can be looked up in a medical dictionary: lupus, Alzheimer's, AIDS, cancer. Sometimes, the name of the sea is sickness.

For some of us, the name of the sea is failure. We are afraid we just are not going to be able to produce. We are afraid we will not quite measure up. Sometimes, the name of the sea is failure.

For some of us, the name of the sea is opposition. We are afraid someone whose smile we long to curry is not going to approve of us. We fear that we might lose the favor of our chosen audience. "Suppose they don't like me anymore?" "What if they don't agree with my position?" Sometimes, the name of the sea is opposition.

For some of us, the name of the sea is money. "How will we pay these bills?" "How can we handle this mortgage?" "How are we going to send the children to college?" "How will we ever be able to retire?" Sometimes, the name of the sea is money.

For some of us, the name of the sea is crime. A company in New York City is selling bullet-proof coats, clipboards, and book bags for grammar school children. Dead-bolt locks are about as common in our city as window screens. We cringe at the headlines and warn our children. Sometimes, the name of the sea is crime.

The sea has lots of names. For some of us, the greatest fear is that we will die before our time, while for others of us the greatest fear is that we will live so long that we will be finally and completely alone. For some of us, the greatest fear is that we are not important and our lives somehow do not really matter. For some of us, the greatest fear is that God is not going to receive us, that somehow things will never be quite right between ourselves and our God. For some of us, the greatest fear is that we will lose the prosperous job, or we will lose the family business, or we will lose contact with our teenager.

There is no shortage of fears. There are as many fears as there are people. Until the day when there is no more sea, there is, in fact, much more sea. There is no shortage of fears, real and imagined. So, what do we do with them? What do we do with our sea? What do we do with our fear?

First of all, we can begin by acknowledging the fact that many of our worst fears never come to pass. Frederick Buechner has somewhere reminded us that usually "neither our greatest dreams or our worst fears come true." Some of us spend a considerable portion of our lives running from enemies that are not hunting us, hiding from troubles that are not haunting us, and dreading diseases that are not hurting us.

I was about eight years-old when my father's father, Eugene Poole, died. My most poignant memory of Daddy Gene is one summer sunset when he and I were sitting on the front porch of the house in Kite, Georgia, where he and Ma Bessie lived. There was a big open field across the road from their house. That evening there were dark, summertime storm clouds way out where the field and the sky conspired to make the horizon. I remember watching the flickering forks of lightning dart from the clouds to the earth. I was scared. I kept thinking Daddy Gene would say, "We'd better go in the house." Finally, I said, "Daddy Gene, don't you 'spect we'd better go inside before that storm comes?" For some strange reason, I remember to this day that old man's red-skinned hand as he put it on my little knee. And then, in the slow rhythm of his sharecropper's voice, Daddy Gene said, "Don't worry about that storm boy. It's goin' go on around. That lightning is a far piece from here."

What Daddy Gene said was true about that far-off thunderstorm, and it was true about lots of other clouds that have piled up on my horizon since then. Some of the storms we fear the most never come. They go on around. The lightning is a far piece away, and the storm that scares us never strikes us.

What can we do with our fears? We can start by acknowledging the fact that many of our worst fears never come to pass. It would, of course, be wonderful if that were always true. But, the truth is, some of our worst fears do come true. Some of the storms do break right on top of our lives. One of these days there will be no more sea. But between now and then, there's much more sea. And sometimes, we really are out there in the sea. The waves cannot be stopped, and the bottom cannot be touched, and the end cannot be seen. Sometimes our worst fears do come to pass. We find ourselves in the sea.

How do you live when you are scared to death? I think you start by telling the truth. It helps to hang words on things that are bigger than we are. Somehow or another it seems, not to vanish the trouble, but to at least shrink it down to its true size. Tell the truth. If you are scared, say so; and be specific. Name your sea. Say what it is that chokes you with dread, sweats you with anxiety, and paralyzes you with fear.

One evening, about two years ago, Maria and Joshua and I went for a walk while Marcia was fixing supper. As we turned the corner of our street, we found ourselves just a few feet away from a loud, roaring tractor. A man was digging the foundation for a new house. The big backhoe was churning around, and dust was flying everywhere. Maria, who was three years-old at the time, clutched my finger in her tiny fist and, in the face of that huge, loud, yellow monster she said, in a trembly little voice, " 'Ria not scared. 'Ria not scared. 'Ria not scared."

Of course, the fact is, nothing could have been further from the truth. "Ria" was scared. That's exactly why she kept saying she was not scared. But if you are really scared, that just does not work. If you are afraid, you are afraid. And all the protests and denials to the contrary will not vanish your fears.

So tell the truth. Tell the truth to yourself. Tell the truth to God. Tell the truth to someone whom you love and trust. Tell the truth. If you are scared, say so. Name your sea. Call your fear by its name. Tell the truth. And then, after you open your mouth to tell the truth, open your life to hear the truth. Tell your truth to God, and let God tell His truth to you.

The truth to hear is that God is with you, not away from you. The truth to hear is that God is for you, not against you. The truth to hear is that God is sustaining you, not forsaking you. The truth to hear is that somehow, somewhere, someway, someday, there is going to be a new, unhindered, unbothered, untroubled life for you in the uninterrupted presence of God where there is no more sorrow, no more pain, no more crying, no more death, and (are you ready for this?!) no more sea!

No more sea? No more anything to fear or dread? Our first response is that it's just too good to be true. But if we know who God is, our last response is that it's too good not to be true.[3] Our first thought is that "no more sea" is too good to be true. After all, there is so much sea. There is so much fear in our world and in our lives. Our first thought is that "no more sea" is too good to be true, but our last thought is that "no more sea" is too good not to be true. It's just like God to make it so that, someday, nobody is afraid of anything anymore.

One day there will be no more sea, no more anything to fear. But between now and the time there is no more sea, there will be much more sea. Between now and that day when there is nothing left to dread, there will be some things left to fear. Many of our worst fears never come to pass. Some of our fears do come to pass and turn out to be not anywhere near as bad as we dreaded all those mid-nights when everyone else was asleep and we were sweaty and awake and scared. Some of our fears come to pass and are every bit as bad as we imagined they would be, but we discover, to our amazement, that God keeps us on our feet, and we live through trouble that we never would have dreamed we could have survived.

One of these days, somehow, somewhere, some way, someday, we will live in the unhindered, uninterrupted presence of God. There will be nothing to fear. There will be no more sea. Until then, there is, in fact, much more sea. But we will not drown in the waves of our fear. Even when we are scared, we know that God is with us, not away from us; for us, not against us; helping us, not forsaking us. That is enough to keep our hearts above water until, finally, there is no more sea. Amen.

Notes

[1]Carlyle Marney, *Recovery of the Person* (Nashville: Abingdon, 1963) 131-33.

[2]Morris Ashcraft, "Revelation," *The Broadman Bible Commentary* (Nashville: Broadman, 1972) 12: 356.

[3]Frederick Buechner, *Telling the Truth* (San Francisco: Harper & Row, 1977) 98.

Chapter 2

If They Only Knew

Psalm 139

I was so good at what I did that everyone thought it came easy to me. If they only knew. If they only knew how hard it was for me. If they only knew what it cost. They thought it was easy for me because I was good at it. But it was killing me. If they only knew.

I think I shall always remember those words. I was in a distant city, sharing a restaurant table with one of the finest preachers in our land. He was prominent, successful, and respected. But he was also very, very weary. As he told his story, that haunting phrase kept coming back around, over and over again: "If they only knew."

If they only knew. It is a quartet of words that, sooner or later, finds a stage on nearly every tongue. Most everybody, at one time or another, has thought, or felt, or said "If they only knew."

There are people who have positions of great prominence and high visibility who are really very private people. They long to be out of the spotlight and away from the limelight. Every now and then they whisper to themselves, "If they only knew . . . Everyone thinks I love being out front. They think I cherish center stage. If they only knew that I am bending my natural temperament completely out of shape to accommodate the demands of this job. If they only knew."

There are people who maintain a constant appearance of security and self-assured control. Others look at them and envy their unruffled confidence. All the while they are running scared on the inside, looking confident and feeling afraid, thinking in the silent shadows, "Oh, if they only knew."

And what about those who carry unmanageable burdens hidden safely out of sight? "If they only knew how bad it hurts. If they only knew how depressed I feel. If they only knew."

And what about those who look at tightly knit circles of friends and mutter to themselves "If they only knew how lonely I am. If they only knew how much I'd like to be included in the group, invited to the lunch, or noticed at the church."

"If they only knew" is a quartet of words that, sooner or later, makes its quiet debut on nearly every tongue:

If my family only knew how unimportant I feel.
If my parents only knew how hard I'm trying to please them.
If our friends only knew how fragmented our marriage is.
If people only knew how you treat me.
If my children only knew how it hurts when I don't hear from them.
If she only knew how much I love her.
If he only knew how much I miss him.

"If they only knew." Very few of us will make it through life without saying it out loud, whispering it down low, or thinking it inside. It is the common phrase that finds a home on nearly every quivering lip: "If they only knew."

We long to be known for who we really are. We want someone to understand us. It is true that we all fear being known because we all have thoughts, feelings, and motivations that we would not want anyone to discover. But, the strange truth is, the only thing that is stronger than our fear of being completely known is our desire for someone to really understand us and to truly know us. We want to be understood. We want someone who is friend to us or kin to us to really, truly know us. It is not even so important that they do anything for us or change anything about us. We just want to be known and understood. "If they only knew."

The fact is, they probably do not know, and they probably will not know. If you have one or two people in your whole life who really know you and understand you, then you have one or two more than many folks ever have. Many people live out their whole lives without ever feeling really known or completely understood. "If they only knew" dies on their lips as a wish unanswered, a hope unfinished, and a longing unfulfilled.

That old southern spiritual song had it right: "Nobody knows the trouble I've seen. Nobody knows but Jesus." Nobody knows. Nobody really knows me. That is the first line of that old cotton-field song. And it is true. If they only knew, but they do not. Nobody knows all the most important things about you.

Everybody knows your name, but who knows the deepest disappointment that scars you? Who knows the deepest joy that thrills you? Who knows the deepest fear that paralyzes you? Who knows the most haunting anxiety that jerks your heartbeat into your throat when you wake up in the middle of the night? Who knows the deepest worst that shames you every time you remember it? Who knows the deepest best that lifts you every time you follow it?

If they only knew . . . , but next to nobody does. If they only knew . . . , but they do not. "Nobody knows the trouble I've seen. Nobody knows . . ." I have about forgotten the rest of that old song. How does it end? "Nobody knows the trouble I've seen. Nobody knows . . . " "Nobody knows . . ." Now I remember: "Nobody knows but Jesus." That is the other half of the song. It is also the other half of the truth about life as a child of God.

The fact is, God knows. God knows. Theologians call it omniscience. Omniscience is a big word that means *God knows everything.* Now, how I hear that depends entirely upon what I believe about God. I mean, after all, if God, in my mind, is an enemy, the idea that God knows everything scares the daylights out of me. "If God knows everything, I never will be able to get God to like me." "If God knows the deepest worst, then I'll never be able to get God to think well of me." If God, in my mind, is an enemy whose favor I am striving to earn, then "God knows everything" strikes quivering fear into the center of my soul. If, however, God, in my mind, is not an enemy whose favor I must curry but a friend whose grace I can trust, then I can rest in the assurance that the God who knows my deepest worst is the God who forgives my darkest sin.

All of us have a few experiences along the way, just a small hand-ful of moments in life, that levy such a powerful "tax on our memory"[1] that we never fully escape the experience or leave the moment behind. One of those lingering moments and enduring experiences came for me several years ago in the tiny prayer chapel of a big city institution.

I walked right past the chapel, but it seemed that something drew me back to the door. I looked in, saw that no one was there, and went down to the front. There, on top of the dark wooden kneeling rail was one of those little white vinyl autograph books with a fancy plastic pen. I figured it was there so folks could sign their name when they came in to pray. It did not have the appearance of privacy about it, so I opened it up. What I found was not just auto-graphs and signatures, but prayers. People had written prayers to God in the autograph book.

I began to read the prayers. Most of them were petitions for sick loved ones. Some were obviously prayers from grieved, frightened, and anxious souls. But one of the prayers was different from all the others. I can close my eyes and still read it on the inside parchment of my eyelids. In the sprawling, uneven handwriting of what appeared to be a teenager there was this prayer: "Dear Lord, please help Mama to get well soon. And Lord, please forgive me for, well, you know, our secret. Amen."

"Please forgive me for, well, you know, our secret." Something was haunting some sensitive soul. "Lord, please forgive me, for, well, you know, our secret." And God does. God does know, and God does forgive. God knows. God knows and God forgives the deepest worst, but that is not all. God not only knows the deepest worst that haunts us. God also knows the deepest best that tugs us. All our secrets are not bad. To the contrary, in fact, some of the secret unknown things hidden inside us are far better than anything that people ever see in our lives.

If God knows the deepest worst that is in us, then God must also know the deepest best that is in us. As surely as there is a deepest worst lurking in us all, there is also a deepest best waiting to step forth. All our secrets are not bad! Some of the secret, unknown things hidden inside you are far better than the best that people have ever seen in your life. There is the affection for a friend that you feel but have never communicated for fear of being embarrassed. There is the liberal generosity that you have always felt but never spent because of limited income and limitless obligations. There is, in each of us, some unknown, carefully hidden, secret best that has only partially found its way out into the open. If they only knew!

I think that I shall always remember sitting across from the late John W. Carlton in his office at the Southeastern Baptist Theological Seminary. The huge brown desk loomed between us. His steely blue eyes pierced the room. With his unrivaled insight and unequaled eloquence, Dr. Carlton said to me, "Chuck, boy, we're all going to die with half our music still in us." John Carlton was right. There is "another half of the music" in all of us. None of us has ever lived out all our noblest impulses. Few of us ever completely incarnate all of our most Christlike intentions.

When Robert Louis Stevenson died, one of his friends offered the magnificent assessment that "Robert died with a thousand stories still inside."[2] What was true of Robert Louis Stevenson is, in some fashion, true of every one of us. We will all die with "a thousand stories still inside" . . . with a thousand kind words unspoken, a thousand noble impulses unobeyed, a thousand encouraging notes unwritten, a thousand feelings of compassion unacted upon, a thousand good secrets untold. If they only knew.

If they only knew the secret you! If they only knew, but they do not. They do not, but God does. God knows the deepest best about you. God knows the deepest worst that shames you. God knows the deepest scar that hurts you. God knows the deepest fear that haunts you. And, God knows the deepest best that tugs you!

We are all going to die with a thousand good stories still inside. Even if we live with uncommon devotion to Christ our lord, we will still probably die with about half our music still in us. But God knows. God knows the deepest best that no one else has ever seen in you. It is only for us to worship God, follow Jesus, and spend our lives making the best music we can, knowing all along that the God who loves us knows every note, measure, and beat of the other half of the music. Amen.

Notes

[1]The phrase "levy a tax on our memory" orginated, I think, from Norman Cousins.

[2]Quoted by John W. Carlton, *The World in His Heart* (Nashville: Broadman, 1985) 25.

Chapter 3

Hard Things Are Hard

Jeremiah 15:18; 2 Corinthians 1:8-11

One morning, a long time ago, I called a friend with whom I had not spoken in awhile. He happened to be at home. In fact, he was at home in bed, quite sick. My friend had one of those high-pressure jobs, the kind of job where almost any decision he made would inevitably affect the lives of others. He had just finished making some of those very hard decisions, and the stress of it all had made him physically sick. We talked awhile about all of that. Then my ailing friend spoke a phrase into the phone that found its way into the center of my life. Summing up the whole story of his heavy burden, my friend said this:

Hard things are hard. Sometimes life is just plain hard. You can't escape it or get around it; you just have to live through it. Hard things are hard.

My weary friend unintentionally uttered the absolute truth in that sick-bed sentence. After all, hard things are hard. You cannot escape life's hard things. There are no detours around them or short-cuts over them. All the power of positive thinking you can muster will not take the hard edge off hard things. All the "silver lining in every cloud" cliches you can recite will not make that which is truly hard into something soft or easy. My friend was right. Hard things *are* hard. From where do hard things come? And what do we do with them when they come to us?

From where do the hard things come? Well, some of the hard things are our own doing. Some of the hard things are our own creations. We make wrong choices, and those wrong choices carry with them their own inevitable, inherent consequences and results. We really do reap what we sow, not because God needs to get back at us, but because our deeds carry their own results. Some of our hardest hard things are simply the inevitable results of our own sin. When we try to be something other than what God created and redeemed us to be, then our wrong choice, our sin, carries with it its own inherent, inevitable results.

So many of the hardest hard things in our lives are the inevitable results of our own wrong choices. If we choose to abuse our bodies, we then live with the hard reality of diminished strength and broken health. If we choose to break our vows of marital faithfulness, we then live with the hard reality of fractured trust and a fragmented life. If we choose to live day after day after day without ever pulling aside from the noise of life to talk to God, listen to God, and to put ourselves where God can have a chance with us, then we will live with the hard reality that there is simply no quiet peace, no clear direction, and no sustaining courage at the center of our soul.

Some of the hardest hard things in our lives are simply our own doing. The pain, the embarrassment, and the alienation that result from our sinful choices constitute some of the hardest hard things in our lives. Hard things are hard, and sometimes the hard things are of our own making—but not always. Not all the hard things can be traced to some sinful choice that we have made. Sometimes, the hardest hard things that come into our lives are things over which we have absolutely no control. Someone else makes a choice, and we get caught in the ripples, or trapped in the shadow, or drowned in the wake of their decision.

Those secondhand hard things are all around us. A madman on the other side of the world decides to oppress his corner of the globe, and a five-year-old boy watches his daddy board a ship for Saudi

Arabia. Hard things are hard. A person with a twisted mind decides to do violence to another human being, and a stunned family carries with them for the rest of their lives the memory of a lost loved one and a scar that never fully fades. Hard things are hard. Someone decides to tell a vicious lie about a rival or an opponent, and a sterling reputation is turned black and blue by the subtle bruise of a rumor. Hard things are hard.

Hard things are hard, and sometimes life's hardest hard things land in the laps of life's most innocent bystanders. Hard things are hard. Some of life's hard things are our own doing; we can trace them to our own sin. But some of life's hard things are the far-flying shrapnel of someone else's tragic choice, the far-reaching ripples of which engulf our lives in uninvited pain. And, then, some of life's hard things cannot be traced to anybody's sin—ours or anybody else's. They just come. And when they come, those hard things are hard.

We can spend our lives trying to decipher the unresolvable mystery of human suffering. We can wrestle with the common question of "why do bad things happen to good people?" We can scan the scriptures with a magnifying glass, seeking guarantees of good health and exemption from trouble. (I have done all of the above!) But the truth is, we live in a world where bad things happen. We live in a world where there are germs, and diseases, and evils. The scriptures simply do not offer us the promise of insulation from pain, isolation from trouble, or exemption from hard things. Hard things are hard. And some of them come, not from a traceable origin, but as part of the mystery of life lived in a world where bad things can, and do, happen.

Some of those hard threads in the fabric of life are little, narrow, hard threads that stay for a day and quickly fade away. Some of those hard threads in the fabric of life are big, wide, hard threads that come to stay and never fade away. Big or little, long or short, though, hard things are always hard. They make you stop at the operating room doors. You listen to your three-year-old crying for you on the way to the tonsillectomy. Hard things are hard. That troubled paleness on the physician's face turns out to be the prelude to some devastating words about the results from last week's tests. Hard things are hard.

The boss says you cannot delay the transfer any longer. Move your family to the new city next month, or find another job. Hard things are hard. You realize that you cannot postpone the layoffs any longer, and you happen to be the person at the top. Hard things are hard. You know the layoffs are coming, and you happen to be the person at the bottom. Hard things are hard.

They call you in the middle of the day to say he fell from the monkey bars and you should meet them at the doctor. It is just ten stitches, but hard things are still hard. They call you in the middle of the night to say she finally gave up the struggle. She was eighty-four and ready to go, but hard things are still hard. The treatments burn his mouth, the nursing home hurts her pride, the doctors say "no hope" about your case, the nurses say "no change" about your husband, the judge says "no parole" about your child . . . and hard things are hard.

So, what do you do? What do you do when hard things are being their hard selves in your life? Perhaps we should matriculate in the classroom of Jeremiah and Paul for an education in how to handle hard things. After all, Jeremiah and Paul majored in hard things. Hard things were really hard for Jeremiah and Paul. They would have unanimously endorsed my friend's assessment that hard things are hard. Jeremiah and Paul lived with hard things, not by pretending they were easy, but by telling their story and embracing their hope.

When Jeremiah and Paul told their story, they made quite a duet. Listen to Jeremiah as he cries out to God about his hard things: "Why is my pain perpetual, and my wound incurable?" And then, like an echo across a canyon, Paul cries back from the other side of the Bible and says, "We do not want you to be ignorant of the affliction we experienced in Asia, for we were so utterly, unbearably crushed that we despaired of life itself."

Paul and Jeremiah knew where to start when hard things were hard. They started by telling their story. Jeremiah told his story to

God, and Paul told his story to his friends. They did not varnish it, dilute it, or pretend that it was easy. They did not try to camouflage their pain in the masquerade costume of evasive denial. They opened their mouths and told their story.

That is exactly where we must begin. You and I must learn the lesson that Jeremiah and Paul would teach us. Tell your story. If hard things are hard, then tell your story as honestly as Jeremiah and Paul told theirs: "O Lord, why is my wound incurable? Why is my pain perpetual? I am so utterly, unbearably crushed that I am in despair!"

If Jeremiah and Paul could go that far with their story, then you can go that far with yours. God has been around for awhile. You are not going to offend God with your story. You are not going to tell God anything that God has not already heard. Do as Jeremiah did, and tell God your whole story. Do as Paul did, and share your story with some trusted someone who will hear you and understand. When hard things are hard, start where Jeremiah and Paul began: tell your story.

That is where you start, but that is not where you stop. When hard things are hard, you begin by telling your story, but you continue by embracing your hope. After Paul told his painful story, he embraced his sustaining hope. Hear his words again:

We were so utterly, unbearably crushed that we despaired of life itself, why, we felt that we had received the sentence of death; but that was to make us rely, not on ourselves, but on God who raises the dead: God delivered us, He will deliver us, and on Him we have set our hope that He will deliver us again.

When hard things were hard in Paul's life, he opened his mouth to tell his story, and he opened his life to embrace the hope that God will do as well in the future as God has done in the past. This is our great hope.

Nothing has ever been more senseless, more evil, or more hard than the crucifixion of Jesus. But God took that darkest of hard things and turned it into the front edge of the greatest of good things. God raised Jesus from the dead. This is God's world. In God's world, the hardest, darkest, worst thing is never the last thing.[1] The God who raised Jesus from the grave will do as well in the future as God has done in the past.[2] Embrace the hope!

When hard things are hard, we begin by telling our story. We continue by embracing our hope. If we will tell our story with honesty and embrace our hope with trust, then we just might be able to do two more things. If, when hard things are hard, we will tell our story and embrace our hope, then we just might even be able to wring whatever good can be wrung from the hardest of hard things and then, having wrung the good out of the bad, walk on with hope into whatever is left of life.

Not long ago, I heard John Claypool tell an unforgettable story about a beautiful plum tree that stood for years in his grandfather's yard. The tree was the prize of the farm. It was the pride of his granddaddy's eye. One day a tornado swept across the southern Kentucky community where the Claypool family lived. The storm twisted that plum tree from its roots and left it lifeless on its side.

After the tornado had blown over, the neighbors began venturing out of their homes to survey the damage. By and by, a few of the neighborhood men gathered in the Claypool's yard. They stood in a silent circle, gazing down at that once-beautiful plum tree, now ruined beyond repair. Finally, one of the men asked John Claypool's grandfather, "What are you going to do with that tree?" After a long pause, the old man replied, "I'm going to pick the fruit and burn the rest."[3]

"I'm going to pick the fruit and burn the rest." That means I am going to wring the good from this sad event and then get on with life. That really is the only honest response to life's wounds, storms, losses, and pains: pick the fruit and burn what is left. When hard things are hard, if we will tell our story and embrace our hope, then we just might be able to pick the fruit from the hard thing, burn the rest, and get on with life.

Pick the fruit: take from the awful experience whatever new sensitivities to others you may have learned. Pick the fruit: take from the dreadful disappointment whatever new insights into life you might have gained. Pick the fruit: take from the painful loss whatever new discoveries you might have made about the sustaining presence of God. Pick the fruit, and then burn the rest.

Hard things are hard. Hard things will find their way into my life and yours. When they come, what will we do? We will tell our story. We will embrace our hope. Who knows, we might even be able to pick the fruit, burn the rest, and walk on with hope into whatever is left of life with the God who raised Jesus Christ from the grave! This is our hope! Amen.

Notes

[1]The phrase, "The worst thing is never the last thing," is attributed to Frederick Buechner (source unknown).

[2]The idea that "God will do as well in the future as God has done in the past" is spawned by a phrase in John Claypool, *Tracks of a Fellow Struggler* (Waco TX: Word 1974) 101.

[3]John Claypool, lecture, Mercer University Theological Institute, Macon GA, April 1990.

Chapter 4

The Things I Cannot Change

Jeremiah 29:1-14

It came as no surprise to me when, a few years ago, I read that, of all the sermons the late Carlyle Marney preached, the one of which the most tapes and printed copies were requested was a sermon called "In the Meantime."[1] (It is also probably the Marney sermon that has been most frequently pilfered, borrowed, stolen, and plagiarized by preachers!)

It was that sermon, "In the Meantime," that first introduced me to this absolutely riveting scripture passage from Jeremiah.[2] This relatively obscure corner of the Old Testament had never held any great attraction for me, but once I stumbled over it in Marney's sermon, I have never been quite able to get away from it. There just might be no other single passage in the whole Bible that more fully captures our common human predicament than this dusty old fragment of the letter that Jeremiah wrote to the children of God who had been carried away captive into Babylon.

Jeremiah wrote a letter to his defeated, weary, captive kin people. It was a letter about the things that could not be changed. The captives had been carried away from their homeland to a strange place. They hated the way their lives had turned out. They only wanted to come back home. But that was not going to happen, at least not for a long, long time. So Jeremiah wrote them a letter about living with the things that could not be changed.

When we read Jeremiah chapter 29, we are reading someone else's mail.[3] After all, the letter was written twenty-five hundred years ago to a crowd of captives in a distant place. It is someone else's mail, not ours. But the longer we read it, the more we get the feeling that it is our mail, not someone else's, because the letter is about something that is mighty, mighty personal to every one of us. The letter is about living with the things you cannot change. To those captives in Babylon, and to you and me, God's advice on Jeremiah's lips is this: "When you're living with the things you cannot change, you will stay most fully alive if you will face the facts, come to terms, and hear the truth."

Jeremiah's initial advice to the captives was "face the facts." "Don't believe those utopian prophets who tell you that things will soon be changing, captivity will soon be over, and you will soon be home," he said. "Don't build your life on those false hopes. Your captivity is going to last seventy years. Things aren't going to be changing any time soon." The word from God for the captives was "face the facts."

Apparently there were some self-appointed prophets going here and there among the people telling them that the captivity was about to end and things were about to change. Jeremiah said, "Don't be taken in by those false prophets with their false promises. Face the facts. This captivity is going to last seventy years. Face the facts. This is not something that is going to be changing any time soon. Face the facts. Some of you will never see home again. Face the facts. This problem is going to last a lifetime."

Jeremiah's facts are mighty hard to face. We usually do pretty well if we believe that the trouble will soon end, or the wound will soon heal, or the hurt will soon fade. And most of the time, that is exactly what happens. But what about the things that will not end, or heal, or fade? How do we live with the things we cannot change? Well, Jeremiah says we start by facing the facts that some things are not going to change.

Jeremiah told those captives that they would be in Babylon seventy years. That's a lifetime. They would never see home again.

Jeremiah said, "Face it. This is not something you can change." He did not advise them to pray harder, or have more faith, or beg God louder. He told them to face the facts. "Life has not turned out at all the way you would have planned it," Jeremiah said. "And it's not going to change. This problem is now a part of your life. Face the facts."

Most of life's problems, illnesses, and burdens pass away rather quickly. But what about the ones that do not? What about the things that just are not going to go away? When we bump into realities that will not move, we have to face the fact that here is something difficult or disappointing, or painful, or sad; and it is not going to go away or get fixed anytime soon. This is something that I cannot change.

Once we face the facts, then we can begin to do the next thing on Jeremiah's list for captives. Jeremiah not only admonished the captives to face the facts about their plight, he also advised them to "come to terms" with their captivity. Jeremiah encouraged the captives to get on with their lives.

It is never enough just to face the facts. Facing the facts isn't where you stop. Facing the facts is only where you begin. After all, you can face the facts about the difficult situation you cannot change and then just quietly fold up your life, and close up your heart, and give up your future. Or you can face the facts about your situation, come to terms with your circumstances, and make the best of your life. That is what Jeremiah advised the captives to do.

"Don't put your lives on hold," he said. "Go ahead and live. Build a house. Plant a garden. Encourage your children to date, fall in love, and get married. Do the ordinary, important, and positive things that matter. Build a house . . . you will be here for the whole thirty-year mortgage. Plant a garden . . . you will still be here when those butterbeans are ready to pick. Let your sons and daughters date and marry . . . if they do not date and marry in captivity, they will never date and marry anywhere. This is it for the next seventy years. If you do not make peace with this captivity and come to terms with it and live in it, you'll never have any peace at all. Come to terms."

Jeremiah warned the captives against putting their lives on hold. I think one of them might have already written a song advocating that sort of posture of postponement. It had probably done real well on the charts. It shows up in the Psalms as number 137. The songwriter said, "We've hung our harps in the willow trees. We won't be needing them until this captivity is over. How can we sing the Lord's song in this strange land?"

But Jeremiah said, "No!" to the captivity blues. Jeremiah said, "If you don't sing in this strange land, you'll never sing anywhere. This is your life for the next seventy years. This strange land is all the land you're ever going to have. So you might as well come to terms with life as it is. It's here to stay. You cannot change it. So come to terms with it. Make peace with your life in Babylon. Build you a house. Plant you a little garden out back of it. Let your sons and daughters enjoy life, and go ahead and enjoy it yourself. After all, this is it. You can either come to terms with life as it is and enjoy it; or you can close up shop, and fold up heart, and wither into bitterness. Come to terms with life in captivity. You can't change it, but you can live fully and freely and faithfully within it. Come to terms."

I have about decided that the only way you and I will ever be able to come to terms with the things we cannot change is for us to begin by acknowledging one simple reality: life, after all, is only going to get so good. Life is never perfectly safe, utterly simple, or totally smooth. There will always be at least a few things that we would change if we could change, but we cannot change. The only way we can ever live life fully, freely, and faithfully is to come to terms with life as it is and make peace with the things we cannot change.

The word of God on Jeremiah's lips for captives then and now is this: We just cannot put life on hold until things get better. After all, things might not get better. We have to come to terms with life as it is, make peace with the things we cannot change, give some of our dreams a decent burial, and make the best of the rest of our dreams that can still come true.

I suppose that must be the meaning of the now-famous prayer of Reinhold Niebuhr. Story has it that Dr. Niebuhr jotted down a few lines for a prayer he was to offer one Sunday at a worship service. Afterwards, someone there asked if they could see a copy of the prayer, which Niebuhr had folded up and put away. Out of his pocket Reinhold Niebuhr drew the lines that have become perhaps the most familiar of all modern American prayers:

> O God, grant us the serenity to accept what cannot be changed, the courage to change what can be changed, and the wisdom to know the difference.[4]

It seems to me that Niebuhr's prayer is an echo and a ditto of Jeremiah's advice. There are some things that cannot be changed. The past cannot be undone. There are bad choices that, once made, cannot be unmade. There are handicaps and diseases that will not be cured in a week, or a month, or a year or ten or twenty. I rather suspect that every single one of us has something in our lives that we would change if we could that simply cannot be changed. We can let that something paralyze us, and control us, and eat us alive. Or we can come to terms with the fact that it cannot be changed, and then get on with life as best we can and enjoy what we can enjoy without letting things we cannot change change us into a bitter, brittle shell of our former self.

Once we face the facts about the things we cannot change, we must then come to terms with the things we cannot change. But even that is not enough. There is something else that we must do in the face of the things we cannot change. After we face the facts about life and come to terms with our circumstances, we must hear the truth about God.

Jeremiah not only advised the captives to face the facts and come to terms, he also admonished them to "hear the truth." He laid the facts plainly before them: "This captivity is not going to end any time soon. This is going to last seventy years. This is something you cannot change." Then, he told them to come to terms with their plight, make peace with their situation, and get on with life the best way they could. But now, finally, Jeremiah speaks the word of hope. He admonishes the captives to hear the truth that is greater than the facts. Jeremiah has given the captives the hard facts, and now he gives them the great truth. Jeremiah says,

> Thus says the Lord: "When seventy years are completed for Babylon, I will visit you, and I will fulfill to you my promise and bring you back to this place. For I know the plans that I have for you," says the Lord, "plans for welfare and not for evil, to give you a future and a hope." (29:10-11)

This is the truth that God sends to the captives on the lips of Jeremiah. The facts are hard: "This captivity is not going to end any time soon." But the truth is great: This captivity will not have the last word. God will have the last word. God will come, and when God comes, God will end the captivity and take His children to their true home. "God," Jeremiah said, "has something in mind for you, and that something is a future and a hope."

Jeremiah not only meant for those poor, weary captives to face the facts about life and come to terms with their situation; he also meant for them to hear the truth about God. The facts about life always have to be faced, but the facts are never all there is. Beyond the facts about life, there is always the truth about God. Frederick Buechner, in his wonderful book *Telling Secrets,* quotes George McDonald as saying "No facts can take the place of truths."[5]

There is a word of truth about God that is always and forever greater than all the facts about life. The word of truth is an outlandish, incredible, magnificent word of hope. It is the Easter-colored affirmation that, "despite all the overwhelming evidence to the contrary,"[6] this is God's world, and God's plan is to give us a future and a hope. This is the truth.

Oh, I know. All the facts say differently. The facts about life are often hard, sometimes frightening, and occasionally devastating. And those facts must not be whitewashed by the thin paint of positive thinking. Those facts must not be buried in the shallow soil of utopian denial. Those facts must be faced, but they must be faced in the light of the truth that is simply more enduring than the facts. To refuse to face the facts about life is to fall into a false hope, but to refuse to hear the truth about God is to fall into a false despair.[7] The truth as God said it and Jeremiah reported it is this: God has not forgotten us. God is always caring for us. God has a plan for us. God's plan is to give us a future and a hope.

The truth is, despite all the evidence to the contrary, this is God's world. The truth is, in God's world, the worst thing that happens to us is never the last thing that happens to us.[8] The truth is, no kind of life, no kind of death, no kind of guilt or sorrow or pain or shame, no kind of anything, shall be able to separate us from the love of God that is ours in Christ Jesus our Lord. That is the truth. The only trouble with the truth is that it can be mighty hard to hear when your ears are full of the facts. When your ears are full of the hard facts about sickness and stress and death and disappointment and sadness and divorce and tragedy and crime and weariness and misunderstanding and sin, then it can be mighty hard to hear the truth about hope and grace and forgiveness and strength.

I figure we hear the truth of hope and grace about like we hear our favorite song on a radio station that is too far away to be clear and too close by to be ignored. You have had that experience. You are out there on the interstate pushing the buttons. You hear, through the interference and the static and the fuzz, the come-and-go, in-and-out lines of a favorite old song you have not heard in a long time. You strain your ears to pick it out from all the other noise. You think to yourself, "This is silly. I could listen to something else on a closer station and hear it fine. But here I am listening to mostly static and fuzz just so I can catch a faint, distant spin of Luke Warmwater singing 'Perched on the Porch with You'." But then you think to yourself, "I'd rather barely hear my favorite song than listen to anything else up close. I'd rather hardly hear my favorite song than not hear it at all."

That's the way it is with the truth. You can hardly, barely, faintly hear the truth of hope and grace when your ears are so full of the facts about all the hard things that you know you cannot change.

But you and I would whole lot rather hear the truth of hope and grace barely than not hear it at all. We would rather hear the truth of God's enduring love hardly than not hear it at all. In fact, about the only way we ever get to hear God's truth is through the static and interference and noise of the undeniable hard facts of life. But even to hear a little of the truth is to know that God has a plan for us.

God told Jeremiah, and Jeremiah told us that God's plan is to give us a future and a hope. If that is true, then that will do.[9] If that is true, then that is enough. If it is true that God is always with us and always for us, then that is enough to color life's darkest facts in the softer shades of Easter-colored light. It is enough to give us the courage to face the facts about the things we cannot change, and come to terms with the things we cannot change, and enjoy life in spite of the things we cannot change.

If the truth that Jeremiah told is true, then it is enough. If it is true that God plans to give us a future and a hope, then that means that ultimately, finally, when all is said and all is done, the last word heard will be hope, and the last thing done will be God's. If that is true, it will do. If that is true, it is enough. If that is true, then you and I can live with hope, and peace, and even joy in spite of all the things we cannot change.

Every one of us is captive to something we cannot change. Our best hope to stay on our feet, and enjoy life, and experience joy, and bless others is to take Jeremiah's advice for captives then and now: Face the facts about life. Come to terms with circumstances. Hear the truth about God. The truth is that God has a plan for us, a future for us, a hope for us, and a home for us. From wherever you stand, you have a future with God.[10] And that is the truth, believe it or not! Amen.

Notes

[1]See William Carey, *A Pilgrim's Progress* (Macon GA: Mercer University Press, 1980) 124.

[2]Carlyle Marney, "In The Meantime," *Pastoral Preaching*, Charles F. Kemp, ed. (St. Louis: Bethany Press, 1963) 65-72.

[3]For the phrase "reading somone else's mail," I am indebted to Fred Craddock.

[4]*Eerdman's Book of Famous Prayers*, Veronica Zundel, compiler (Grand Rapids MI: Eerdmans, 1983) 37. The story about the prayer is circulated in various "apocryphal" versions.

[5]George McDonald, *Curate* (New York: Routledge, 1876) 490-91, as quoted by Frederick Buechner in *Telling Secrets* (San Francisco: Harper, 1991) 204.

[6]Frederick Buechner, *A Room Called Remember* (San Francisco: Harper & Row, 1984) 34.

[7]Marney, "In the Meantime."

[8]The phrase, "The worst thing is never the last thing," is attributed to Frederick Buechner (source unknown).

[9]Joseph Sittler, *Gravity and Grace* (Minneapolis: Augsburg, 1986) 63.

[10]Marney, "In The Meantime."

Chapter 5

The Porch Is Never Empty

John 5:1-9

S he died more than one hundred years ago, but with the passage of time her name has grown more familiar, her work more revered. Much of what she wrote never saw the light of day until after she died. She is alternately treated by historians as an eccentric hermit, an original rebel, and an ingenious poet. She was "the belle of Amherst," Emily Dickinson. Of her dozens of sonnets and odes, none speaks more accurately to the human predicament than the sonnet that begins "Heaven is what I cannot reach." Emily Dickinson was right, was she not? "Heaven is what I cannot reach" was Emily Dickinson's unforgettable way of saying that so often the thing we want most in life dangles just out of reach.

I guess no one has ever understood that frustrating fact any more clearly than the poor fellow whose tale is told in John chapter five. Every day, all day long, "Heaven was what he could not reach." For thirty-eight years, "Heaven was what he could not reach." The thing he wanted most was wholeness and health. Wholeness and health always dangled just out of reach for the helpless man who lay on Bethesda's porch.

His helplessness was compounded by his loneliness. The other sick folks on Bethesda's porch had strong sons to assist them, or faithful daughters to move them, or quick neighbors to carry them.

He had no one. He had no friend to help him down to the water. Every time he started out, somebody else beat him to the water. He watched and watched. Sometimes the village boys hid behind the wall and threw rocks to make cruel ripples in the pool and trick Bethesda's congregation of cripples. Sometimes he imagined the water was moving, when it was only a breeze-flung shimmer of sunlight teasing on the surface.

False starts at the wrong time . . . heroic struggles to race to the water at the right time . . . it was no use. Something always went wrong on his way to the water. The realization of his fondest dream and his strongest desire dangled elusively, just out of reach. He had waited all those years for things to work out. He had lived a solitary life: friendless, helpless, always waiting for things to change, dreaming of some far-off someday when life would finally be happy, simple, and easy.

Then, one day Jesus went walking on that troubled porch with its capacity crowd of crippled, paralyzed, powerless people. He was drawn to this one man. To this one man Jesus said, "Rise. Pick up your little pallet. Walk." The man was healed. He found his dreams fulfilled, not in the magic bubbles of a mysterious water, but in the surprising presence of a mysterious stranger who gave him strength in his body and courage in his heart to stand on helpless feet and walk on powerless legs.

Bethesda's porch offers an unforgettable and inescapable commentary on life in the real world. Life in the real world is captured and framed in the snapshot of Bethesda's porch. In the real world, some people receive the miracle. They receive the brightest answers to life's darkest questions. They find the absolute fulfillment of their most ambitious dreams. In the real world, sometimes we are given the miracle for which we have prayed, and longed, and waited. Just like the man who danced and skipped the length and breadth of Bethesda's porch, we receive the fondest desire of our lives, and everything works out just as we had hoped. We leave the porch with singing in our heart and laughter on our lips.

But sometimes, in the real world, we are not the healed and happy soul who leaves the porch to sing and laugh. Sometimes we are all those other people in the porch-crowd snapshot. Sometimes we are the ones who stay on the porch to wait and wonder and struggle and hope. Sometimes we are left trying to make sense of life on Bethesda's porch. Sometimes we are like the disappointed medical doctor in Thornton Wilder's play *The Angel that Troubled the Waters*. That little one-act play was based, as you might have guessed, on this Johanine scripture lesson.

Wilder enlarges the porch cast to include another character, a physician. The doctor has come to the pool after many years of bearing a terrible burden of shame for a past sin. He is standing beside the pool just as the angel is poised to start churning up the waters. The physician sees the angel and begins to plead with him: "My work grows faint. Heal me, long-awaited angel. Heal me that I may continue." But the angel says,

> Draw back, physician, this moment is not for you . . . Without your wound where would your power be? It is your very remorse that makes your low voice tremble into the hearts of men. The very angels themselves cannot persuade the wretched and blundering children on earth as can one human being broken on the wheels of living. In love's service only the wounded soldiers can serve. Draw back, physician. Draw back.[1]

The physician was so disappointed. He knew what he wanted. He wanted to be released from his pain. He wanted to be happy and carefree. But he was told to draw back from the healing water. He was told to stay on Bethesda's porch. He was a better person with his wounded heart than he would ever have been without the pain. It was his wounds that made him able to identify with other people's pains. It was his scars that enabled him to help people whom no one else could help. It was actually best for him and those around him if he remained on the porch. He was worth more to the world with his pain than without his pain.

If I'm the person who is still on the porch, if I have been to the edge of the healing waters, only to be told "draw back, it's not your moment," then it may be that I am a better person with my infirmity than I would be without it. Perhaps my greatest potential lies in my greatest wound. (That is not to imply that God "sends" us trouble to make us better. Trouble comes to us because we live in a world where bad things happen. But those "bad things" often become the means by which our edges are softened, our minds are opened, and our hearts are strengthened. We become better than we would otherwise have been.)

The day after Easter in 1916, a group of Irish nationalists launched a fervent uprising against the British. The British army met the insurgents, and soon the streets of Dublin were reddened with the blood of young Irishmen. A few months later, in September of 1916, William Butler Yeats wrote a poem called "Easter 1916," commemorating that tragic day. At the close of three of that poem's four verses, Yeats uttered the same haunting phrase: "A terrible beauty is born." Yeats was declaring that those deaths were not useless and those lives were not wasted. Yeats was convinced that what looked like defeat and humiliation was in fact the beginning of something powerful and good. It was terrible, but it was the birthing of a new unseen beauty. "A terrible beauty is born."

There is a powerful, useful beauty that is born in the most terrible corners of Bethesda's porch. I am convinced that is the central pulsating meaning of the magnificent Bible verse in Romans 8:28: "All things work together for good to them that love God and are called according to His purpose." That does not mean that everything that happens is good. That does not mean that everything that happens is sent to us from God or laid on us by God. It does mean, though, that God is at work to bring good out of every event and circumstance in our lives. Paul was saying that God works with us to wring the good from whatever happens to us, to find "the saving possibility"[2] in all circumstances, disappointments, pains, and mysteries.

We live in God's world. In God's world, life is not a riddle to be conquered, a puzzle to be solved, or a test to be passed. To live by faith is to live with mystery. To live by faith is to live in the "key next door" tense of life. Leslie Weatherhead once told about going to look at a house for sale. He went alone to the vacant house and found it all locked up. He peeped in the windows on all sides of the house. He could see some things, but the details of the house remained largely a mystery. He was about to leave in frustration when he saw a small sign in one of the windows, a sign that said "KEY NEXT DOOR." He had to go a little farther down the road to obtain a key that would unlock the doors and reveal the mysteries of the house.[3]

You and I live in the key-next-door tense of life. For you and me, the key is next door. Life is trimmed in the bewildering borders of mystery. We do not understand why some people never get to leave Bethesda's porch. We do not understand why we have to spend so much of our lives waiting for something to go away, or come back, or change, or improve, or start, or end. We live in the key-next-door tense of life. We are not obligated to understand everything. We are not even obligated to pretend to understand everything. Farther down the road, there is the key. Next door, in the nearer presence of God, perhaps we will receive greater understanding. (Or, perhaps, we will find our questions impertinent when we live in the unhindered presence of God.)

Bethesda's porch is life's waiting room. It is a place where people wait for things to get better. Bethesda's porch is where people wait for health to return. Bethesda's porch is where people wait for the pain to go away from their back, or their legs, or their head, or their neck, or their hands. Bethesda's porch is where people wait for the fifth of five chemotherapy treatments. Bethesda's porch is life's waiting room. It is where people wait for a better job, a higher salary, a happier marriage. Bethesda's porch is where people wait for the problem to be resolved, the trouble to go away, the depression to end, the grief to cease, the embarrassment to fade, the controversy to die.

The porch is never empty. We have all sat with our feet dangling off the edge of Bethesda's porch, waiting for things to work out. We are not strangers to the longing and yearning of Bethesda's porch. When we are left on the porch, it helps to remember that the key is next door. When we are stuck on the porch, it helps to understand that this is God's world, and in God's world, a terrible beauty is always being born. A terrible beauty is being born, even on Bethesda's porch. Amen.

Notes

[1]Thornton Wilder, *The Angel that Troubled the Waters*, as quoted by L. D. Johnson, *The Morning after Death* (Nashville: Broadman, 1978; Macon GA: Smyth & Helwys, 1995) 100.

[2]Source unknown.

[3]Leslie Weatherhead, "Key Next Door," *The Twentieth-Century Pulpit*, James W. Cox, ed. (Nashville: Abingdon, 1978) 269-77.

Chapter 6

How Long?

Psalm 6; 13

How long? "How long?" is a question you hear in cars. Over and over again, little voices from the back seat, asking the same question every 2.7 miles: "How much further? How long 'til we get there?"

How long? "How long?" is a question you hear in homes. "How long until supper is ready? How long will you be gone this time? How long before these installments will be paid off? How long is it going to take you to get dressed?"

How long? "How long?" is a question you hear in churches. "How long do you think this sermon is going to last?"

How long? "How Long?" is a question you hear in hospitals. "How long will the surgery take? How long will she be in intensive care? How long will the cast stay on? How long before he can eat? How long before she can go back to work? Doctor, how long do you think he will live?"

If you live long at all, your lips will form the yearning syllables of the common question, "How long?"

How long can we keep this marriage together?
How long can I live with this pain?
How long before the newspapers will leave us alone?

How long can I keep going like this?
How long before this house will sell?

"How long?" is a question for all people and all times. Our mentor in the dialect of "How long?" is the "how long" psalmist. No one ever asked "How long?" with greater intensity than the psalter poet. Listen to him. He has stood about all he can stand. Life is just too much for him. He is drawing back the curtain of his soul. The mask of his heart is falling to the stage. He is telling God the truth. He is asking God for help. And we get to listen. But when we eavesdrop on the psalmist, we hear more than the desperate musings of an ancient poet. We hear the intimate dialect of people we love. We hear the familiar echoes of our own most difficult moments and demanding struggles.

Listen to the weary sister or brother who wrote the how-long psalms. With stooped shoulder, muted laugh, slowed step, and moist eye, the psalmist peeks out from beneath the wide gray paw of suffocating trouble. She moves her lips to intone the language of despair:

How long, O Lord? How long is life going to be like this? I am tired, O Lord. I am tired of worrying. I am tired of being afraid. I am tired of being embarrassed. I always wake up in the night. I never can go back to sleep. I make my bed swim with tears. I inundate my pillowcase with tears. I irrigate my mattress with tears. How long, O Lord, how long? How long, Lord, will you forget me? Forever? How long is my life going to be like this? How long? How long? How long?

Why was the psalmist so miserable and weary? What fear, what pain, what sorrow, what embarrassment made his mattress float in a bath of midnight tears? What do you think? What makes you cry "How long?" to God? What keeps you awake when you wake up in the night and the digital radio carves a pale blue 2:47 AM into the side of the darkness? What could make you bathe your face with tears and soak your pillow with weeping? What could make you wonder if God was hiding from you and forgetting about you? What makes you stare up to God with yearning eyes and call out to God with trembling lips, "How long?"

We should probably pause right here to remember that there are some times in our lives when we ask "How long?" not because life is too hard to bear, but because life is too good to last. "How long can life be so easy? With all the tragedy and suffering in this world, how long can me and mine be spared? How long can the business prosper? How long can my husband stay in good health?" These are not the questions of pessimistic paranoia; these are the questions of honest realism. The "why me" questions get a lot of publicity, but sometimes, life's great question is not the "Why me?" of bitter despair, but the "Why not me?" of grateful wonder.

Occasionally, "How long?" is an expression of wonder over the ease and joy of life. But usually, "How long?" is a testimony of fatigue and despair.

Sometimes, we ask God "How long?" because of sickness:

"How long, O Lord, must my mouth burn from this chemotherapy?"

Sometimes, we ask God "How long?" because of weariness:

"How long, O Lord, can I keep up this ridiculous pace?"

Sometimes, we ask God "How long?" because of boredom:

"How long, O Lord, must I stare at these same four block walls and smell these same nursing home smells?"

Sometimes, we ask God "How long?" because of shame:

"How long, O Lord, until I can look in the mirror without feeling this awful load of guilt?"

Sometimes, we ask God "How long?" because of fear:

"How long, O Lord, until I can be awakened at three in the morning and not have knots in my stomach?"

Sometimes, we ask God "How long?" because of embarrassment:

"How long, O Lord, how long will I keep recalling my stupidity, rehashing my immaturity, reliving my mistake?"

"How long?" is the universal interrogative. "How long?" is the common question. "How long?" is the inevitable inquiry. Sooner or later, we will all give our own echo to the psalm. When we are living in the shadows of weariness, shame, humiliation, or fear, we hold hands across the centuries and make a duet of the psalmist's solo. "How long?" we ask. "How long?" we plead. "How long?" we demand.

What can we do when the minor-chord music of "How long?" becomes the theme song of our life? We can remember, first of all, that most of our troubles do have an end. This is not escapism; it is realism. When you are paralyzed in the middle of great difficulty, it seems that it will last forever. But the fact is, time does pass and troubles do end. Wounded pride heals. Shame goes away. Grief's pangs become less frequent and severe. Fears dissolve. Wounds close. Controversies fade. Time does pass. Time does not heal all wounds, old cliches not withstanding. Time does not heal all wounds; God heals all wounds, but God usually heals us within the context of the passage of time. Most of life's "how longs" are answered, simply by the things that happen in the passage of time.

Baptist educator and theologian Kirby Godsey has wisely written, "Human life cannot be lived in advance."[1] There is, sometimes, simply no substitute for the passage of time. Time is one of the instruments of God's healing grace for fractured bones and fragmented spirits, wounded bodies and broken hearts. Many of the "how long" question marks will be replaced by an exclamation point of hope, or a period of resolution, or at least a comma of relief with the passing of time.

But what if "How long?" turns out to last a lifetime? What about the person who, like Abraham, "dies not having received the promise?" Sometimes, people die with an unresolved "how long?" on their lips. We cannot explain, explain away, or understand the life-long pain that some must bear. We are not even obliged to pretend to understand. We are not even required to mouth cliches that profess understanding. In the face of life's unanswered "how longs," all I know to do is to put my life in the hands of the God whom we know in Christ Jesus. God can be trusted.

The late L. D. Johnson's wonderful book, *The Morning after Death,* ends with these words:

God can be trusted! In the last analysis, Christians have no more persuasive word. God can be trusted. That does not resolve all the mysteries or answer all the questions, but it gives us enough to build our lives around. God is trustworthy. He is Lord of life and death and He is to be trusted.[2]

God can be trusted. The "how long" psalmist learned that lesson. He concluded his litany of despair with a rousing descant of trust. The poem that began "How long wilt thou forget me O Lord? Forever?" ended like this: "I have trusted in thy mercy; my heart shall rejoice in thy salvation." The psalmist's question rightly has a place on our lips. We do ask, "How long?"—we have before, and we will again. But the psalmist's confession must also find its home in our hearts and on our tongues. God can be trusted. God raised our Lord Jesus from the grave. "God is Lord of life and death, and God is to be trusted."

Before we go, I have a few questions for you, a few "How long?" questions.

How long will . . .
> *God listen to you?*

How long will . . .
> *God be at work in your life?*

How long will . . .
> *God mean to do you good?*

How long will . . .
> *God remember your finest moment?*

How long will . . .
> *Christ Jesus our Lord be your Savior?*

How long will . . .
> *the Holy Spirit be your Comforter?*

How long will . . .
> *God accept you, forgive you, and save you by God's grace?*

How long will . . .
> *God believe in you, and stand with you, and hold you up with God's unwearied strength?*

How long will . . .

God make a place for you at God's everlasting table where life is unhindered, uninterrupted, unbounded, and free?

How long? If you answered "Forever!" move to the head of the class. Amen.

Notes

[1]R. Kirby Godsey, "Living in the Light of Love," unpublished manuscript.

[2]L. D. Johnson, *The Morning after Death* (Nashville: Broadman, 1978; Macon GA: Smyth & Helwys, 1995) 147.

Chapter 7

If You Wait
Until You're Strong ...

Psalm 137:1-4; 2 Corinthians 12:7-10

We meant to make no music: We leaned our guitars in the corner behind the bed. We buried our harmonicas in the bottom of the sock drawer. We boxed up our songbooks and closed up our hymnbooks and folded up our sheet music. We hung our harps in the willow trees.

We meant to make no music. We hummed no tune. We sang no song. Life had turned out all wrong. We were in exile. Our lives had been interrupted by trouble that we had never dreamed would come to us. We could not understand the way things had turned out. We saw no sense in singing until things got better. We hung our harps up in the limbs of the willow trees, because until things changed, until we were strong and happy and home again, we meant to make no music.

Whoever he or she was, the writer of the psalm meant to make no music until things got better. Until things improved, until he got back home, until life changed, until he was happy again, he meant to make no music. She just sat down on the ground and wrote herself a song about not singing. He was putting life's music on hold until he was strong again.

Most of us probably find ourselves right at home with the author of the psalm. He was waiting for things to change. He was waiting until he was strong again and happy again and home again before striking up a tune again. Until his life got in order, he was putting things on hold. We understand. We have done the same thing in the past, or we will do that in the future, or we are living that way now.

We are waiting until our wounds are healed, our questions are answered, our sins are conquered, our mysteries are solved, our turmoil is settled, our doubts are resolved, and our faith is strong. Then we will sing the Lord's song. Then we will do the Lord's work. Then we will bear the Lord's grace to the hurting and the troubled and the lonely and the lost. We are not ready yet, because our own lives are not completely straightened out. So we have hung our harps in the willow trees. We will take them down and go to making music when things get better. We are waiting until we are strong.

There is just one thing wrong with that: If we wait until we're strong, chances are we will never get done waiting. If we are waiting until we are strong and well and happy and holy and secure before we begin giving ourselves away, singing the Lord's song, and touching wounded lives, then we are going to spend our lives waiting on a train that never quite comes in. We will never begin bearing the grace of God to those who need it most if we wait until we are strong. After all, is anyone ever perfectly strong, completely happy, or absolutely holy? Is anyone's life ever totally calm, straight, together, and uncluttered?

I keep remembering an obscure king in the Old Testament. His name was Joram. Joram was ruling the land during a time of severe famine. One day he was out for a walk, strolling the top of the wall that surrounded his home. Two women were on the sidewalk outside the wall, lamenting their starvation. When those desperate, dying women saw King Joram and began telling him the horrors of their plight, the king, in an act of sorrow, anger, and despair, ripped open his robe. Then the people in the street saw that, underneath his king suit, Joram was wearing another suit, a second suit, a hidden suit. It was a suit of sackcloth. King Joram was wearing a hidden suit of sackcloth next to his skin—sackcloth, the universal uniform of the sad and sorrowful. Joram ripped off his public, visible suit, and underneath there was a private, invisible sackcloth suit of sorrow.

Joram's "second suit" has become, for me, a parable of life. Sometimes those who look strong on the outside are wearing a hidden suit of sackcloth where no one else can see. They look so happy. They seem so secure. They appear so strong. But, like the king in the story, their despair is traveling incognito. Their sackcloth vest of sorrow is well-hidden beneath their camouflage suit of strength.

I am not so sure that anyone in this world is ever going to arrive at that utopian station of bliss where they are completely happy, absolutely holy, or perfectly strong. If we are waiting until we are perfectly strong to sing the Lord's song, touch wounded lives, and give ourselves away, then we just might be waiting for a train that never quite comes in. Oh, we may look mighty strong and secure and independent on the outside, but we will probably always wear at least a little vest of sackcloth hidden away where no one else can see.

And anyway, whoever said we have to be strong all the time? In fact, we might actually be worth more to God and other people in this world with our wounds than without them. Remember Jacob, the Jacob who keeps popping up over and over again in the first book of the Bible? Jacob was left with a limp after an all-night encounter with God. The truth is, Jacob was a much better person with his limp than without it. Perhaps we all walk best when we walk with a limp.

Remember the confession of the apostle Paul? "Three times," he said, "I asked God to take away this thorn in my flesh. But God would not remove it. God gave me grace to live with it, and I have learned that when I am weakest on my own, I am strongest with God." Paul was better with his thorn then he was without it. He was more sensitive with his wound than he was without it. He was stronger with his weakness than he was without it.

Does that mean, then, that God sends trouble or sickness or turmoil or pain upon us in the hope of making us better? I think not. If you adopt that posture, you will have to seriously rethink your understanding of who God is and how God acts. The fact is, if you live in this world, trouble or sickness or turmoil or pain will, in large measure or small, come to you. It comes, not because God sent it to you or laid it on you or aimed it at you, but because that is just the kind of world in which we live.

But out of the fiery trial and pressing clutch of trouble or sickness or turmoil or pain, we do become softer of heart, quieter of step, more humble of spirit, and more sensitive of soul. In our weakness, we become strong. God's grace and presence somehow seem to flow more freely through our broken, dependent lives than through our unscathed, self-sufficient lives. Thus, like Paul, when we are weakest, God really is strongest.

One of the truly wonderful ministers of this century was William Edwin Sangster. Dr. Sangster, who died in 1960, was an outstanding Methodist pastor, preacher, and leader in Great Britain. From 1929 to 1932, Sangster was pastor of two churches in Liverpool. His ministry there met with resounding success. During Pastor Sangster's years in Liverpool, both of his pastorates flourished, and both of the two sanctuaries were filled on Sundays. Yet, after Dr. Sangster's death, his son Paul found in some of his father's old papers a journal entry from those Liverpool days that indicated that all was not well inside the soul of this very successful minister. The great minister wrote these words on a paper dated September 18, 1930:

> I am a minister of God, and yet my private life is a failure in these ways . . . I have lost peace . . . I have lost joy . . . I have lost taste for my work . . . I feel a failure.[1]

William Sangster was not perfectly strong. He was, in fact, limping on the inside. The shoulders of his heart were stooped and bent and slumping low. And yet, his ministry was being wonderfully used to bear grace to the people of Liverpool. We could look at his mixture of success and pain and say, "What would he have been able to do if he had been perfectly happy and completely confident and totally strong?" Who knows. He might have done less. It might, after all, have been his weakness and pain that made him such an honest and sensitive bearer of grace.

We just cannot wait until we are strong. For one thing, very few folks are ever completely and absolutely strong in this life. And for another thing, it is nowhere written that we have to be strong to be useful. In fact, to the contrary, we may run our greatest races and deliver our finest gifts while stumbling with a limp.

We cannot wait until we are strong. You and I cannot wait until all our wounds are healed, all our questions are answered, all our sins are conquered, all our doubts are resolved, and all our turmoil is settled before we begin to sing the Lord's song, give ourselves away, and bear grace to the broken lives around us.

While you and I wait until we get stronger or better or happier or holier, the poor wait for a check that never gets written, the lonely wait for a visit that never gets made, the discouraged wait for a note that never gets mailed, the shut-in waits for a call that never gets dialed, and the sad wait for a casserole that never gets baked.

We simply cannot hang our harps in the willow trees until everything is just right in our lives. We cannot put life on hold until we are strong. If we wait until we are strong to begin helping the weak, mending the broken, lifting the fallen, and bearing the grace, then we will never get started at all. We either go ahead and serve other people out of our own weakness, or we sit and wait for some far-off elusive someday when everything is finally all right in our life.

But, the fact is, that day never comes. If we do not sing the Lord's song in a strange land, we will never sing it at all. We just cannot wait until we are strong. After all, who ever said you have to be strong all the time? After all, God said that God's strength most often flows most freely through our weakness.

If we wait until we are strong to begin giving ourselves away, singing God's song, and touching wounded lives, then we are going to spend our lives waiting on a train that never quite comes in. And while we are waiting for a train that is not coming, that measure of God's music that only we can make lies silent and unsung.

So limp on over to the willow tree, unhang your harp, and get to playing. We need your music now. We cannot wait until you are strong, and neither can you. Amen.

Note

[1]Paul E. Sangster, *Doctor Sangster* (London: Epworth 1962).

Chapter 8

I Saw Your Face, and It Looked Like God

Genesis 33:1, 4, 10

There he comes. You can hardly see him. It is so early in the morning that the grass is still wet enough to make the cuffs of his pants turn dark with dew water. You do not have to ask him if he slept any last night. You can look at him and tell. His eyes have narrow red lines through the center and wide dark circles around the rim. He has a pine straw napping in his hair and a sandspur sitting in his beard. He has red clay on the knees of his pants. He has swamp mud clinging to his shoes.

He's walking with a bad limp, struggling up the hill from the creek bank where he spent the night. He looks like he has been in a fight or something. That is because he has been . . . in a fight or something . . . he is not sure. All night long he wrestled with something he could not see. He has been fighting the air. He has been rolling on the ground: down to the edge of the creek, up to the top of the bank, on his feet, on his face . . . fighting, wrestling, rolling all night long . . . no sleep, no rest, nausea, trembling, heart pounding . . . filled with dread and fear and regret and shame and anger. It is like his whole life was captured in this mysterious stranger with whom he fought all night long.

Jacob had longed since midnight for day light to send the darkness away. But he had dreaded the dawn because today was the day he had to face the one from whom he had been running most all his life. Just over that hill was Jacob's brother Esau. Esau hated Jacob, and he had good reason to hate him. Esau, who had sworn that he would have his revenge someday, was waiting over the next hill. And Jacob was limping to meet him. So many years ago, Jacob had deceived their daddy Isaac into changing the will. Jacob had taken advantage of his old daddy's diminishing powers and had gotten him to change the will so that it favored him over his older brother Esau.

Now, after all these years of living with the guilt and the fear and the alienation and the separation, Jacob was about to meet Esau for the first time since that awful day when Esau swore that he would have his revenge. And what made it so bad was that Jacob knew that he had done wrong. Even if he had not sprained his hip in the midnight creek-bank free-for-all, he still would not have had a leg to stand on. Jacob was wrong, and he knew it. Jacob was scared, and he looked it. Jacob's heart was pounding in his neck with the dread. Esau was waiting over the hill.

And now he sees him. Jacob gazes across the field. There are people all around. Esau's four hundred soldiers and servants are gathered in a clump. Jacob's family and animals are over in the other side of the pasture. And there is Esau . . . big as ever, bigger than life, standing in the grass, staring at the brother he has not seen since that awful day twenty years ago when Jacob tricked their daddy into changing the will.

Jacob took a deep breath and headed straight towards the man from whom he had run in fear and shame all these years. He did not get far, though, before Esau started towards him. Esau, who swore he would kill Jacob if he ever got his hands on him, was about to get his hands on him! He got his arms on him too! He took Jacob in his arms, and held him to his chest, and hugged him in his grasp, and kissed him on the head, and wept in his hair. And Jacob's dread and fear and shame and guilt shook out in sobs of relief and unbelief. When Esau let go of Jacob and Jacob found his voice, he said to Esau those unforgettable, inescapable, magnificent words: "I saw your face, and it looked liked God."[1]

What did he mean: "I saw your face, and it looked like God"? Earlier in Genesis we learned that Esau was a big, hairy fellow who grew a beard and stayed out in the fields all the time. Does Jacob mean to say that God has a big neck, bulging biceps, bushy sideburns, and a tan? No. Jacob did not say God looked like Esau. What he said was that, for a minute there, Esau looked like God. He said,

When I saw your face, it was like looking at God. The way you embraced me and took me in your arms and kissed me and . . . it . . . it shocked me . . . I . . . I don't know. When I saw your face, it was like looking at God. I saw your face, and it looked like God.

When Jacob saw Esau, he saw an unexpected hug. When Jacob saw Esau, he saw an unbelievable reception. When Jacob saw Esau, he saw unearned forgiveness, undeserved love, and inexplicable acceptance. Jacob knew what he deserved from Esau. He knew what he had coming. And now all those years of dread and fears of fury were swept away by an unexpected hug, an unbelievable reception, an unearned forgiveness, and undeserved love.

Have you ever known anyone who looked like God? Is there anyone in your life who looks like God to you? The people who look like God are the people who understand us, believe in us, bless us but do not curse us, hug us like Esau, love us like God, and make us want to be better. The people who look like God are also the ones who are with us for God and keep us on our feet. They take the noun friend and turn it into a verb. They "friend" us. They are with us for God, and they keep us on our feet. Who is it that looks like God in your life? Who believes in you for God and makes you want to be better?

And what about you? To whom does your face look a little like God? Do not blush and deny the resemblance. If you have ever gotten your eyes off yourself, gotten yourself off your hands, and put your life in God's hands, then you have probably looked like God to somebody, somewhere, sometime. If you have just read the Gospels and then asked God to help you do what Jesus would do if he were here, then more than likely you have looked like God to somebody. Now, you cannot look like God to everybody. You cannot even look like God to lots of folks. But if you are spending your life, investing your life, giving yourself away, then to somebody out there, you look like God. Oh, they know that God does not look like you! But they saw your face one day, and, for a minute there, it looked like God.

They had made a dreadful choice or a stupid mistake or a sinful decision, and they knew that tongues were wagging and disgrace was all around. You came to them with grace—just grace. You gave them an unexpected hug and an unforgettable word of hope. You came to them with grace, and for a minute there, you looked like God.

They were sitting alone for three hours in a hospital room, waiting for the surgeon to call and tell how it went. You came in the door with a cheeseburger, an orange drink, and time to sit. For a minute there, you looked like God.

They just got back from the funeral home, picking out the casket and setting the time for the service. You had cleaned their house and cut the grass before all the out-of-town family started coming in. For a minute there, you looked like God.

They had just gotten her home from the surgery and got her into bed when they heard the doorbell. You were standing at the screen door with a casserole, some biscuits, and a pie. (You were hoping they'd hurry because the potholders were thin and the casserole was hot.) When they got to the door and saw you, for a minute there, you looked like God, juggling your tupperware and your pyrex dishes on the front step.

They see you most every Sunday at church, but every time they see you it makes them feel good. You always bless and do not curse them. You squeeze their hand. They look across the room or meet you in the hall, and, for just a minute there, you look like God.

Oh, do not worry. They know God does not look like you. They are not going to worship you or confuse you with God. They know that God is not like you. It is just that, sometimes, you are so much like God. When you are with people for God, when you greet a person with the embrace of unexpected acceptance and unearned affection, when you listen, listen, listen, to them and hold them up and friend them, then when they see your face, it looks like God.

No one can look like God for everyone. In fact, you are not going to look like God for most people—you cannot. But you must look like God for someone. When you look like acceptance, when you look like forgiveness, when you look like understanding, when you look like real help for real needs, when you look like real love for the real world, then you look like God. People see your face, and it looks like God. Imagine that! Amen.

Note

[1]This idea was spawned for me by a published sermon of Carlyle Marney's, "A Come and Go Affair."

Chapter 9

The Strange Gift of Grief

1 Thessalonians 4:13-14

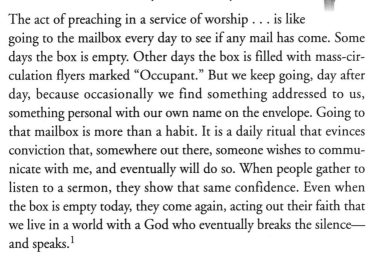

One of this generation's most insightful teachers of preachers is Thomas Long, a professor at Princeton. In his book, *The Senses of Preaching,* Dr. Long offers this wonderful description of the experience of hearing sermon after sermon, Sunday after Sunday:

> The act of preaching in a service of worship . . . is like going to the mailbox every day to see if any mail has come. Some days the box is empty. Other days the box is filled with mass-circulation flyers marked "Occupant." But we keep going, day after day, because occasionally we find something addressed to us, something personal with our own name on the envelope. Going to that mailbox is more than a habit. It is a daily ritual that evinces conviction that, somewhere out there, someone wishes to communicate with me, and eventually will do so. When people gather to listen to a sermon, they show that same confidence. Even when the box is empty today, they come again, acting out their faith that we live in a world with a God who eventually breaks the silence—and speaks.[1]

And so it is. We keep "going back by" the church house, hearing sermon after sermon, week after week. Sometimes, there is not a whole lot there for us, but there have been times when there has been something personal—a word from God "with our own name on the envelope." It has happened often enough that we would never consider not going back by the place of meeting where hymns are sung and sermons are preached.

Whenever the sermon is about grief, everyone's name is on the envelope. Any honest word about grief uttered in any sanctuary on any Sunday from any pulpit is a piece of personal mail for everyone in the house. When the sermon's subject is grief, the homily is a letter with everyone's name scribbled across the front. After all, no one fully escapes the shadow of grief. Grief is the great democratizer: everyone who lives, sooner or later, grieves. "Grief is the aftermath of any deeply felt loss."[2] Since we all experience losses large and small, we all feel grief now and then. Grief comes early. Grief stays late. We will all know the pain of grief.

In our sanest, highest, most mature moments, we know that grief, even with all its pangs and pains, is a blessing, not a curse. We may even someday come to look upon grief as a gift from God—a strange gift, perhaps, but a gift nonetheless. (This is not to say that the loss that occasioned the grief is a gift. We must be careful to make a critical distinction between the loss that devastates us and the process of grief that follows the tragic loss.) Who knows . . . it just might be that one of the clearest expressions of real progress and maturity as a follower of Christ is an emerging capacity to see grief (even grief!) as a gift from God, a strange gift that somehow enables us to recover from the losses that bruise and shatter our lives.

When we finally enter the unhindered, uninterrupted, unending presence of God, there will be, in the words of the Revelation, "no more grief." The reason there will be no more grief is that there will be no more loss. We won't need the gift of grief anymore because our lives will not be disrupted by loss anymore. But as long as money, jobs, health, homes, friends, children, husbands, wives, parents, siblings, and dreams can be lost, we will need the strange gift of grief. It is the painful gift that becomes, not a place to stand and hurt, but a path to walk and recover. The strange gift of grief takes different shapes in different lives. But if we reduce the gift of grief down to its least common denominator, we can probably say that, for all of us, grief is love's inevitable price, life's lingering echo, and hope's best chance.

Grief is love's inevitable price. If we love deeply, then it is exceedingly likely that we will, eventually, grieve deeply. I think there was a country song that sort of summed it up with these words: "I could have missed the pain, but I'd a'had to miss the dance."[3] Whoever wrote that line landed mighty close to the truth. The only way to miss grief in life is to miss love in life. Grief is love's price. About the only way to never grieve is to never love, but to never love is to never fully live. The only way to miss the pain of loss is to miss the whole dance of life. Grief is love's inevitable price. Grief is the price we pay for loving deeply.

Sometimes, late at night, I go to the door of Joshua's room, gaze down at his sleeping face, and wonder if there will be a Korea or a Vietnam or an Iraq to take him when he is twenty the way so many others have been taken at the edge of adulthood. Sometimes, I stand at Maria's door, look at that tiny sleeping face, and wonder if someday the twists and turns of life will bring pain and sorrow to her when she is a woman.

Wherever you have parents and children, you have the immense promise of joy, but you also have the enormous possibility of grief. Wherever you have husbands and wives, you have the immense promise of joy, but you also have the enormous likelihood of grief. Wherever you have intimate friendship, you have the immense promise of joy, but you also have the enormous chance for grief. Grief is love's inevitable price. That child on whom you depend might move clear across the country. That friend you cherish might forget you someday. That spouse, whom you love more than life itself, will someday die. If we love deeply, then we will eventually grieve deeply.

To love someone fully, freely, and faithfully is to make yourself completely vulnerable. If you love, you will grieve, but that is no reason to stop loving. Grief, after all, is not a curse. Grieving will not kill you. It is, rather, not loving that will slowly, systematically, kill you. If you do not make yourself vulnerable, take the risks, and love, then you will tragically, sadly, miserably "under-live"[4] life. Grieving is an inevitable part of being fully alive and living in love, but the risk of grief is no reason not to love.

Grief is just the inevitable price we someday pay for a lifetime of intimacy, joy, and love with friends, parents, children, siblings, and spouses. If you love deeply, you will grieve deeply. Grief is love's inevitable price, but that is not all. The strange gift of grief is love's inevitable price, and it is also life's lingering echo.

Most of us knew the late Grady Nutt as one of America's most famous and beloved humorists. A close friend of the Nutts' told me that, a few years after Grady's death, his wife Eleanor said, "The first year after Grady died, my grief was my companion. At least I had my grief."

Eleanor Nutt hung simple words on profound mystery and made perfect sense. "My grief was my companion. At least I had my grief." Grief is life's echo. Grief is—in some strange, mysterious fashion—the last, long, lingering tie that binds us to the one whom we no longer have. I don't understand this, but I know that it is true. Our grief is a gift from God for which we can give thanks; because our grief, even though it hurts, is one last, precious, lingering tie that binds us to the person for whom we grieve.

This is hard to hear and hard to say. This is difficult to understand and impossible to explain, but I know that it is true. Our grief, even our grief, is a gift from God for which to be thankful, because grief is life's lingering echo. The grief we feel for the person we lost is the lingering, binding echo of our relationship with that person. We can no longer touch them, see them, or feel them, but we can remember them, miss them, and grieve them. We are bound to them by the last tie that binds: the pain of grief.

This is at the core of my emerging conviction that grief, while it may be a strange gift, is nonetheless a gift, a good gift from God, a good gift for which to be thankful. Oh, to be sure, the memories hurt. The brittle yellowed stationery, the black-and-white photos, the empty chair at Thanksgiving and Christmas . . . to be sure, the memories fill our hearts with pain and wet our eyes with tears. The grief hurts. But what would we prefer? That God would give us the capacity to forget? Would we rather that God had given us the capacity to completely erase from our heart and mind the life and love that is now gone? If you and I had the choice, I believe that we would rather have the capacity to remember and feel grief than the power to forget and feel nothing. Grief is a gift. Grief is a gift from God. Grief is a gift for which to be thankful. Grief is a good gift because it is life's echo. Grief is the last, lingering, come-and-go-and-come-again echo of the life of someone whom we loved deeply and miss greatly.

Caution: When we define the gift of grief as "life's echo," we must attach a warning label to our words. This sermon needs a blinking yellow caution light right about here. Just as any of God's gifts can be abused and misused, the strange gift of grief can be abused and misused. We can easily "fall in love with the darkness" and decide that we enjoy being pitied more than we enjoy being happy. To spend all of life saying "poor me, poor me" because we want others to say "poor you, poor you" is to trivialize and misuse the strange gift of grief. The strange gift of grief can be as easily distorted as any of the other gifts that God gives. If we only live for the echo of a beloved voice that is now silent, we will miss all the other new voices and living sounds that God gives us. We must never become so enamored with "life's echo" that we cease listening to what life has left to say.

C. S. Lewis said,

> The one prayer God will never answer is the prayer for an "encore." God's creativity is much too vast for that. God simply will not give us back the good old days. God will give us good new days.[5]

Grief is life's echo. It is a gift that binds us loosely to the good old days, but we cannot live on echoes and shadows. We must come to terms with unalterable realities and move on to the good new days, believing that God will do as well in the future as God has done in the past.[6] This brings us to grief's final and crowning mission. Grief is love's inevitable price, grief is life's lingering echo, and, finally, grief is hope's best chance.

Grief is, in some strange, inexplicable, indefinable way, hope's best chance. Perhaps this is the strangest strangeness of all about the strange gift of grief. Of course, the opposite can be true. In the times of our greatest grief, we can close up shop and grow bitter, if we choose. We can decide that we are exceptional, that no one else has ever been hurt or divorced or betrayed or left or widowed or diagnosed. We can choose to write off God and life as absurd and senseless. Grief can be the occasion of that kind of choice.

But there is another far better, far more honest choice. It is the choice to put our lives in God's hands and cast ourselves upon God's grace. Our grief can drive us to God. Our grief can, and does, somehow surgically open up our lives to the God of goodness and grace and hope. Somehow our grief seems to put us where God can have a chance with us. We are thrust by our grief onto something deeper than our trouble, greater than our despair, more enduring than our pain.

Some of us have no time for God when all is well, but then our world is disrupted—the center moves. The once-stable ground of life shifts beneath our feet. Everything comes apart. Someone we loved more than life itself is gone. And in the darkness we open our lives to God. Grief, strangely enough, becomes hope's best chance.

Does all this mean that God sent the trouble to make us turn to God? I think not! No. Trouble comes because we live in a world where bad things happen. Trouble comes because we live in a world in which diseases rage, germs ravage, and people die. God does not whimsically send the trouble to get our attention, but when the trouble comes, God works in our lives. We are so much more open to God when we are grieving than when we are comfortable. Sometimes, grief becomes God's best chance to come into our lives with grace and hope.

Remember what Paul said to the Thessalonian believers? He said, "We don't grieve the same as those who have no hope. We grieve, but we grieve differently. We have hope. God raised Jesus from the dead.

God took what looked like the worst defeat in the world and turned it into the greatest triumph of all." We grieve, but our grief is amended by the hope that God, who raised Jesus from the dead and brought order out of chaos and triumph out of defeat and joy out of pain, will do as well in the future as God has done in the past.[7]

Grief is the common experience of all people. No one eludes the shadow of grief. We will all know the pain of grief. The pain of grief hurts. But in our most honest, sane, authentic moments we know—even if we will not admit it, even when we cannot say it—that grief is a gift . . . a strange gift, perhaps, but a gift nonetheless . . . a good gift at that . . . a gift for which to be thankful. Grief is love's inevitable price. Grief is life's lingering echo. Grief is hope's best chance. Grief: one of God's good gifts for life's hard times. Amen.

Notes

[1]Thomas G. Long, *The Senses of Preaching* (Atlanta: John Knox Press, 1988) 93.

[2]Wayne Oates, *Your Own Particular Grief* (Philadelphia: Westminster, 1981) 15.

[3]"The Dance," written by Tony Arata, performed by Garth Brooks (Hollywood: Capital Records, Inc., 1989).

[4]Walter B. Shurden, unpublished sermon.

[5]C. S. Lewis, quoted by John Claypool, lecture, Mercer University, Macon GA.

[6]John Claypool, *Tracks of a Fellow Struggler* (Waco TX: Word, 1974) 101.

[7]Ibid.

Chapter 10

Don't Cry Past Tuesday

2 Samuel 12:2-24; Ecclesiastes 3:1, 4;
1 Thessalonians 4:13-14

Chances are you never knew J. W. Spruce. He died in April of 1956. Mr. Spruce was a deacon at the Corinth Primitive Baptist Church on Beech Avenue in Macon, Georgia. He woke early one morning with an awful heaviness in his chest, a pain that was the harbinger of his imminent death. His daughter wept as she knelt by his side. J. W. Spruce looked into her tear-streaked face and offered her an unforgettable piece of advice:

> *I can't tell you not to weep. I'd cry too if it was you who was dying. I know you need to cry. But this is Friday morning. So, whatever you do, don't cry past Tuesday.*

"Don't cry past Tuesday," a poignant admonition from a dying father to his grieving child. "Go ahead and cry. I know you need to. But just don't cry past Tuesday."

All of us need to cry. There is most definitely a time to weep, but there is also a time to rejoice. There is a time to mourn, but there is also a time to dance. There is a time to give hope a chance to outrun our grief. There is a time to come to terms with the things we cannot change, and stumble forward in the directions of life and hope.

Our Old Testament lesson from Samuel lets us eavesdrop on King David plunged into the darkness of grief. The king cannot move. He is paralyzed with sorrow. He presses his face to the floor in despair. But then, there comes a day when he rises to his feet, changes his clothes, and eats his supper. There comes a time when King David comes to terms with loss and moves on in hope.

Bathsheba had borne the child of their adultery. Now the baby was critically ill. As the infant struggled for life, David labored in agony—praying, fasting, and grieving for a solid week. After seven days, word came that the baby was dead. The servants did not know what to do. How could they tell the king? How could they report the death of the child over whom David had agonized so fiercely?

David heard them whispering out in the hall. He saw their pale expressions, their downcast eyes. He said to them, "It's the child, isn't it? He's dead, isn't he?" "Yes," the servants said, "Word just came. The child is gone." With that news, the king rose from the floor. He took a bath, changed clothes, ate some food, and went to worship. The servants were bewildered. One of them finally got his courage up and asked the question they all were thinking: "King, when the child was alive, you fasted and mourned and wept. When the child was dead, you ate and bathed and worshiped. We don't understand that."

The king's reply is an intriguing confession of the resolution of grief and the reorganization of life. David did not cry past Tuesday. He came to terms with his loss and moved on with his life. "As long as the baby was alive," he said, "I agonized in the hope that he might survive. But now, he is gone. I can't bring him back. It's over, and we must move on from here." The king's answer is a study in resignation and reorganization. "It's over," he said. With that he went to comfort Bathsheba. Not only did David dry his own eyes, he also went to wipe the tears from another weeping face.

While we might envy the apparent simplicity of David's acceptance of loss, we can hardly assume that such a straight-ahead grief process is the common experience of sorrowing persons. Everyone experiences grief. Grief is an inevitable part of every human life.

Grief is our response to the disruption of our world by any acute loss.[1] Grief can arise from the loss of a job, the loss of physical or mental heath, the loss of a marriage, the loss of security, or, as in the case of King David, the loss of a loved one. No one is spared grief.

Grieving generally follows a path of process. Clinical studies of grieving persons have produced a number of helpful books and articles on the stages of grief. Generally, those stages begin with the stage of shock, sometimes referred to as numbness or blunting. The stages of grief continue, generally speaking, with some combination of denial, anger, regret, depression, and finally, reorganization. Each stage is important. The stages of grief may not be easily recognizable or precisely predictable, but they do describe, in a general way, the pathway that most of us will walk on the way to the resolution of our grief and the reorganization of our life.

For most of us, moving through grief and reorganizing our lives is more like a long, slow, bewildering, multi-tempoed waltz than the straight-forward two step of King David. We need not assume King David as our model of recovery. But David's resolution of grief, even if it cannot be emulated or imitated, still holds for us a valuable lesson: There does come a time when we must come to terms with life and go on with living. All of us will suffer some painful loss in the course of our lifetime. The issue is not whether or not we will weep. We will weep. We will cry. Our task is somehow to learn what David knew, to learn how to come to terms with reality, live into our pain, live through our pain, and then live beyond our pain. The word is not "Don't cry." We will cry. We must. The word is "Don't cry past Tuesday."

But how do we do that? How can we come to terms with loss, do honest business with grief, re-invest our emotional capital, and keep moving? How can we cry without crying forever? How do we keep from "crying past Tuesday"? I am not sure that there is any one absolute answer, but here are a few suggestions that at least lean in the direction of recovery.

We can acknowledge that grief is not one simple, well-chiseled feeling, but a process of weeks, months, and probably years that will likely include the come-and-go feelings of numbness, denial, anger, regret, helplessness, and relief. We can talk to a friend, a minister, or a professional counselor about our feelings. It really does help to "hang words" on our pain and force our sorrow to the dimensions of language.

We can join King David in forcing ourselves, at the appropriate time, to return to the job, the church, the table, the routine. There is healing and recovery in our return to the normal activities of life. We can remember that the pain will likely come, and go, and come again. Grief comes in "pangs." Just as no one is happy all the time, neither is anyone sad all the time. Old pictures, special holidays, favorite songs—these are long-term grist for the mill where grind the pangs of grief.

We can invest our lives in comforting others. As David went to help Bathsheba, so can we go to others with "casseroles and Kleenex." The apostle Paul told the Corinthians that we are to "comfort others with the comfort with which we ourselves have been comforted." If we wait until we are perfectly well and happy to help others, then we will never help anyone. We can go to the hurting and help them while we ourselves are still walking with a limp. Indeed, it may be our limp that makes us effective bearers of grace to the hurting! We can remember that we do not have to be strong all the time. We must open ourselves to the kindness and support of those who love us. We do not have to always be strong! We do not even have to pretend to always be strong.

When our little Maria was nearly three years-old, she was going down the stairs holding Porky the ceramic turtle, Candy the faithful doll, and some unnamed stuffed animals of dubious ancestry. I looked at Maria's tiny, over-burdened arms and asked if I could carry her down the stairs. She replied, "No Daddy. I can carry myself." Sometimes, we cannot carry ourselves. Sometimes, we need to stop acting strong, acknowledge our bruises, and let the people who love us carry us. (Then, someday, we will be well while they are hurting, and we can reciprocate the support.)

Finally, we can claim our hope. We do not have to "cry past Tuesday," because the crowd at the cross did not have to cry past Sunday. They cried Friday. They cried Saturday. But then they laughed.[2] God had raised Jesus from the grave. The very worst defeat in all the world became the most wonderful triumph of all time. As Carlyle Marney once said, "The end of everything became the edge of everything." This is our hope. We live by faith. Our grief is amended by hope, hope made certain and real by the resurrection of Jesus the Christ from the grave.

We will cry. Make no mistake, in this real hard world, we will cry real big tears. Our grief is not annulled by hope. Our grief is not canceled by hope. Our grief is not vanished by hope. But our grief is amended by hope. The dark fabric of our grief is hemmed in the outlandish, enduring, Easter-colored lace of hope—hope made certain and real by the resurrection of Christ our Lord. We will cry, because we cannot escape grief. But we will not "cry past Tuesday," because our grief has been eternally amended by hope. This is God's world. In God's world, there is a resurrection for every death.

So go ahead and cry, but don't cry past Tuesday; because when all is said and all is done, the last word heard will be hope, and the last thing done will be God's. There is a time to weep, so go ahead and cry. And there is a time to laugh, so don't cry past Tuesday. Amen.

Notes

[1] This treatment of grief is heavily influenced by L. D. Johnson, *The Morning after Death* (Nashville: Broadman, 1978; Macon GA: Smyth & Helwys, 1995).

[2] This phrase was spawned for me by a series of sermons that C. Welton Gaddy preached several years ago at Mercer University, Macon GA.

Chapter 11

After Easter: What Is Death for Those Who Live?

2 Corinthians 5:1-8; Philippians 1:21

I almost did not stay today! When I picked up my worship prompter this morning and saw the sermon title, I almost went home. I mean, after all, "what is death for those who live?" That is a bit much for the Sunday after Easter!

What is death for those who live? That might be more than any of us bargained for on the Sunday after Easter. But, if we can stand it, it is a question that needs to be asked. What is death for those who live? What is death for you? What is death for me? What is death for those of us who sit in church on the Sunday after Easter? It is a well-nigh unmanageable question. Perhaps we would do well to split it in two, and make that one ponderous interrogation into a pair of smaller inquiries.

First, what is the death of others for you? Not, "What is your own death for you?" But, "What is someone else's death for you?" Specifically, what does the death of someone whom you really love and need do to you? What happens to you when death interrupts your human relationship with someone whom you love more than life itself? What is the death of a beloved other for you?

Sometimes, the death of someone whom we love more than life itself leaves us feeling devastated. We couch the language of that devastation in questions that sometimes sound like this:

"How can I live without him? We've been married two thirds of our lives."

"How will I make it without her? She always balanced the checkbook. She paid the bills. She knew where everything was. She took care of everything. How can I make it without her?"

"What will I do now? I never realized it, but my strongest motivation to do well was my desire to make him proud of me. Now he's gone. So what do I do now?"

Sometimes the death of a beloved other feels like devastation. Sometimes the death of a beloved other leaves us feeling cheated.

"Why couldn't my mother live to see her grandchildren like everyone else's mother? It isn't fair."

"Why couldn't my daddy live long enough to see me make good, so I could make him proud of me? It isn't fair."

"Why couldn't our child grow up and outlive us like everybody else's child we know? It isn't fair."

The other day I was reading that triumphant passage in 1 Corinthians 15 where Paul wanders off into his magnificent hymn of hope. Remember what he says? "Oh, death, where is thy sting?" I must have read that a hundred times in my life. But this time, for the first time in my life, when I read that, I said to myself, "Paul, I'll tell you where death's sting is. It isn't hard to find. The sting is the feeling that you got cheated." The sting is not hard to locate. The sting of death sometimes feels like devastation, and sometimes it just feels so unfair.

Sometimes, the death of a beloved other leaves us with the feeling of devastation. Sometimes, it leaves us with the feeling that we've been cheated. And sometimes, it leaves us feeling empty—just plain empty—just very, very, tired, speechless, and motionless at the center of our soul. Emily Dickinson could write about death like no one before or since. She laid hold of that deep emptiness for us when she bequeathed to us that row of words that goes like this:

> The bustle in a house the morning after death
> Is the solemnest of industries enacted upon earth
> Sweeping up the heart and putting love away
> We shall not want to use again until eternity.

Emily D. was right. Sometimes someone's death leaves us just emptied out. We don't sweep up our whole heart. But we do sweep up a large corner of our heart, and we put that corner of love away, not to be used again in this life.

The death of someone whom we love more than life itself can leave us feeling devastated, or cheated, or empty. And, strange paradox of life, the death of someone whom we love more than life itself can leave us feeling relieved. That is hard to say. We fear being misunderstood. We do not want to sound unloving. But the fact is, sometimes, the more we love, the more relieved we are for the beloved one who dies at the end of a long, long siege of illness, weakness, and pain.

Is it not strange that the very death that we so long flee as an enemy becomes, someday, a friend? When illness, weakness, and pain stretch from weeks, to months, to years, we cross over some invisible, indistinguishable, indefinable line. Death ceases to be an enemy to be fled and becomes, instead, a friend to be embraced. Sometimes, the death of someone whom we love more than life itself is relief. We cry, but we also sigh. It is over—relief.

This is not simple. We love life in this human body and in this present world. "Because we value life so highly, we resist death so vigorously."[1] We affirm the words of Dylan Thomas who wrote, "Do not go gentle into that good night. Rage, rage against the dying of the light." And rage against death we do. But sometimes, in the long slow struggle with endless, terminal illness, we find ourselves, as

Baptist theologian Richard Francis Wilson has said, "having to hold on to both rage and surrender."

We echo Dylan Thomas' words of resistance, "rage, rage, against the dying of the light," and at the same time we hold hands with Emily Dickinson's words of surrender, "I could not stop for death, so he kindly stopped for me." We rage against the death of our beloved others. And rage we should with medicine, with prayer, and all the weapons of spirit and technology we can seize and wield. But sometimes, we find that we have ceased to prolong life, and, instead, we have begun to delay death. We know it is time for rage to become hopeful surrender. And when death comes, we feel, alongside our sorrow, the strangest feeling of all: relief.

What does a beloved other's death do to those of us who live? Sometimes, it leaves us feeling devastated. Sometimes, it leaves us feeling cheated. Sometimes, it leaves us feeling empty. Sometimes, it leaves us feeling relieved. Sometimes, it leaves us feeling all of that and more.

The other half of the question is this: "What is my own death for me?" What is my own death for me, as long as I live? As long us we live, our own death, rightly understood, holds in its hands two significant gifts. The second best gift that my own death can give to me while I live is a healthy sense of urgency and an appropriate measure of insecurity. If the honest acceptance of the certainty of our own death infuses our lives with a healthy sense of urgency and an appropriate measure of insecurity, then we will have wrung from death her second finest gift.

By "urgency" I do not mean to suggest a frantic, frenetic, high-intensity approach to life. A physician friend of mine once said to me, with great wisdom, "Life, after all, is a marathon and not a dash." To live with a healthy sense of urgency is not to turn the marathon of life into a mad dash. It is not to live a frantic, frenetic, high-intensity, here-and-there kind of life.

We often say, "Live each day as if it were the last day of your life." But before those words have even left our own lips and landed on our own ears, we know good and well that if we lived each day as if it were our last we would never get a thing done. Half of us would not show up for work. We would spend every day hugging people and saying goodbye and fine-tuning our funeral arrangements! It just would never work for you and me to live each day as though it were our last, but it would transform our lives if we would live each day as though someday is going to be the last day.

To live each day as though someday life is going to end is to live with a healthy sense of urgency and an appropriate sense of insecurity that makes us treat life for what it is: a precious, passing, limited gift from God. No one, for me, has ever voiced that healthy insecurity any more clearly than a writer from Texas named Mary Connell.

Mary Connell wrote a poem called "Final Sightings" in which she offered the poignant, brilliant, and moving observation that everything will finally happen for the last time. Her poem forces us to acknowledge that there will be a last time when our child will climb into our lap. There will be a last time when you will carry your son up the stairs or say prayers by your daughter's bed. There will be a last time when the whole family will be together at Thanksgiving. There will be a last time when you will squeeze her hand in the middle of church. Mary Connell pulls it all together with these words:

> And so it is with every sweet occurrence
> That lends any sense or comfort to our lives
> The ultimate gaze and the final phrase
> Is pretty hard to recognize.
> It will happen for the last time
> And very likely no one will know
> When it happened that it stopped happening
> So kiss me every time you go
> Against returning so obscure
> For even though I think I know a certain thing
> I can't be sure.[2]

Those words constitute, for me, a magnificent statement of the second best gift that those of us who live can wring from the certainty of our own death. The second finest gift that death can give to us is the gift of healthy insecurity and appropriate urgency. If you and I come to a place in our lives where we really believe that there is going to be a last time for everything we do, then we will live differently. If somehow, or another, at the center of your soul, you can receive the gift of healthy insecurity, you will live differently. And that gift of healthy insecurity is always ushered in on the arm of an honest acknowledgement of this fact: "I am going to die. There is a limit to my lifetime in this human body."

You don't have much time over which you have any control. Most of your time has already been doled out to work, church, family, and all sorts of other obligations. You only have a small slice of time in your life that is yours about which to make choices. But if you develop a healthy sense of insecurity and an appropriate sense of urgency based upon the acknowledged reality of the limits of the time of your life, it will change the way you look at, and work with, and spend out that little narrow strip of time over which you happen to have some control.

The second best gift that our own death can give us while we live is a healthy sense of insecurity. "So kiss me every time you go, against returning so obscure, for even though I think I know you'll be back, even though I think I know we'll have other times to worship together, to laugh together, to sing together, to eat together, even though I think I know all that is certain, I can't be sure." You cannot, can you? Someday will be the last day. To know that at the center of your soul is to live with the second best gift that our own death can give to us, the gift of healthy insecurity and appropriate urgency.

But the first best gift that our own death can give us while we live, the first and finest best gift, is the gift of hope. The apostle said, "For me to live is Christ and to die is gain." To die is gain because to die, to be absent from this body, is to be present with the Lord. And to be present with the Lord is to have a continuing personal existence in some new, free, unhindered, uninterrupted, unending kind of life.

To be absent from the body is to be present with the Lord, and to be present with the Lord is to be where God is—where they need no candle, where they turn no calendar, where they weep no tear, where they fear no disease, where they watch no clock, where they wait no death. To die is gain because to be absent from the body is to be present with the Lord. This is the enduring, undying hope of the Christian gospel. The first and finest gift that my own death can give me while I live is, irony of ironies, the gift of hope.

In the shadow of Easter, I believe that to die is to go and be where God is, where life is unhindered, uninterrupted, unbounded, and free. "Death, be not proud." This is God's world, and in God's world there is a resurrection for every death. So, death, be not proud. Amen.

Notes

[1] L. D. Johnson, *The Morning after Death* (Nashville: Broadman, 1978; Macon GA: Smyth & Helwys, 1995) 104.

[2] Mary Connell, "Final Sightings," *From The Skin In.*

Chapter 12

The Last Word Is Hope

John 11:21-32

Well, once again, it is time for us to return to the scene of the sisters. You know, those two sisters who sort of pop up every now and then in the Bible. You bump into them here and there in the New Testament. One is named Martha. She is the busy, hard-working one. The other is named Mary. She is the quiet, deep-thinking one.

We have visited with the sisters before. Usually, we talk about how different they are from one another. Why, you would never know they were sisters by looking at them. They usually do not bear much resemblance to one another. Martha you can hardly see. She is a blur of activity. Mary, on the other hand, you can hardly find. She is hiding somewhere, reading a Eugenia Price novel and listening to dentist-office music.

Martha is as busy as a bee; Mary is as still as a stone. They usually do not look at all alike. Mary looks out the window, sees the birds, and watches the sunset. Martha looks at the window, spots a smudge, and grabs the Windex. Mary sits in a chair and lets the ceiling fan's hum lull her to sleep. Martha stands on a chair and cleans the dust off the ceiling fan blades. Martha and Mary. Mary and Martha. They are sisters, but you would never know it by looking at them. They do not look at all alike. Well, except for today.

Today the sisters look like sisters. Today, in fact, the sisters look like twins. For the first time in their lives, the sisters look just alike. In fact, when you look at Martha and Mary today, they not only resemble each other, they resemble you. And they look like me. They look exactly the way we look when life is hard and things go wrong. Martha and Mary look exactly the way we look when we are disappointed that God did not protect us from the sorrow, shield us from the trouble, and save us from the pain.

When you look at the faces of the sisters, you see yourself all those times you have felt more than one emotion. You see a lot of sorrow that Lazarus is dead. You see a little anger that Jesus is late. You see faith. You see doubt. You see disappointment. You see hope. You can catch a glimpse of many emotions on the faces of the sisters. When we listen to Martha's and Mary's words and look at Martha's and Mary's faces, what we hear and see is ourselves when life does not turn out at all the way we had it planned.

Shhh . . . Here they come now. The sisters are coming. Look. They look like you. They look like me. Their faces are our faces. Their words are our words. Here come the sisters. If you look real hard, it is a lot like looking in a mirror.

Needless to say, Martha was the first to get to Jesus. The Bible says that Mary sat still, but Martha met Jesus out at the city limits. It was there that she said those unforgettable words, "If you had been here, my brother Lazarus would not have died." In a little while, Martha went to get her sister, Mary. When Mary saw Jesus, she said the very same thing Martha had said: "If you had been here, my brother Lazarus would not have died." Mary and Martha sound just alike: "If you had been here, my brother Lazarus would not have died."

What do you suppose those words meant on the lips of Martha and Mary? All we get is the words. If we could hear their tone of voice, it would help. All we get is the syllables. If we could hear the accents and pauses, it would help. After all, "If you had been here, my brother Lazarus would not have died" is a distant train of words that can haul more than one freight of meaning.

If you had been here, our brother would not have died. In your ears, how does that sound? How many different emotions can you hang on the pegs of those words? Depending on how you are feeling right now and what is going on in your own life, you might hear those words as a powerful confession of faith. "If *you* had been here, our brother would not have died. Jesus, if *you* had been able to get here before Lazarus died, we know *you* could have made him well. We know *you* would have made everything all right. Oh, we had doctors and preachers and friends and nurses and lots of fine folk here, but there was no one here with your power. If *you* had been here, our brother would not have died."

When you read it that way, the sisters' shared sentence is a confession of their faith in the power of Jesus. It sounds like a compliment: "We know, Jesus, that if it had worked out where you could have come, you'd have been able to do what no one else could. If you had been here, yes-siree, our brother would not have died."

If you put the accent on the right syllables, the sisters' sentence sounds like a compliment. But you can treat the words a little differently, and what first sounded like a compliment takes on the tone of a complaint. The same sentence that sounds like faith's affirmation can also sound like anger's rebuke: "Lord, if you had *been here*, our brother would not have died. Where have you been? We sent word to you that Lazarus was sick. We just knew you'd come on as soon as you got the message. We waited and we waited. But you didn't get here. Lord, if you had *been here*, if you had been where we needed you when we needed you, we'd still have our brother. Lord, if you had *been here*, our brother would not have died."

We do not get to hear the accents, pauses, tone, and volume. "Lord, if you had been here our brother would not have died." We can watch those words stretch across the page, but we cannot hear their syllables rise and fall. Was it an affirmation of faith? "Lord, if *you* had been here, our brother would not have died." Or was it an angry rebuke? "Lord, if you had *been here*, our brother would not have died."

I guess those are two of the furthest extremes on the spectrum. One extreme would define the sister's sentence as a word of confidence in Jesus' presence: "Lord, I'm so glad you're here. Looking back on these past few days and our inability to save Lazarus, I know that if *you* had been here with all *your* power and love, why, Lazarus would have made it." The other extreme would define the sentence as a word of complaint about Jesus' absence: "Lord, where have you been? Where were you when we needed you? If you have *been here* things would be different. Lazarus would have made it, if you had been present. But you were absent."

Well, needless to say, between those two extremes of faith and anger there are other options. We could say, for instance, that the sisters' sentence was just the regretful sigh of "if only." "If only things had worked out differently. If only Lazarus could have hung on till you got here. If only you'd been here. If only things had turned out better."

We could also say that the sisters' sentence was an honest announcement of their disappointment. Maybe they were just disappointed. It is not hard to hear disappointment in that haunting string of the sisters' words: "Lord, if you had been here, our brother would not have died. We're just sad. We're just sad, Lord . . . just disappointed and sad."

"Lord, if you had been here, our brother would not have died." It could have been faith. It might have been anger. It may have been regret. Perhaps it was disappointment. Or maybe, just maybe, the sisters' sentence was a hint at a faint hope. After all, Martha did put a footnote to her sentence. After Martha said, "Lord, if you had been here, my brother would not have died," she did attach a footnote in small type at the bottom of the sentence. Martha said, "Lord, if you had been here my brother would not have died. But I know that even now, whatever you ask, God will give."

Martha did add that little footnote of hope. "I know that even now, something good might happen." It is a hint of hope. Now, let us not go overboard at this point. Martha was not shouting hope; she was whispering hope. After all, she immediately back-pedals from this far edge of personal hope to the safer domains of theological affirmation: "Well, I know Lazarus will live again out there in eternity at the resurrection day."

Martha is not shouting hope; she is whispering hope. After all, it is Martha who tries to keep Jesus from doing something embarrassing when she says "Oh no, Jesus. Don't have them roll the stone from the tomb. After all, he's been dead four days. The odor will be awful. Let's not try this." Martha is no shining example of unmixed hope. She is not shouting hope. But maybe when the sisters say, "If you had been here, our brother would not have died," maybe they are saying, "Now that you *are* here, who knows. Something good may yet happen." Maybe they are whispering hope.

Well, it is kind of hard to tell, is it not? The sisters' sentence might be faith's affirmation, or it might be anger's rebuke, or it might be something in between: a sigh of regret, a tear of disappointment, or a whisper of hope. "Lord, if you had been here, our brother would not have died" could have carried any of those emotions when it left the lips of the sisters and found the ear of Jesus. The sisters' sentence could have meant any of those things: faith, anger, regret, disappointment, or hope. The distant train of their dittoed, echoed, identical sentence could have carried the freight of any of those feelings. Or, you know what? It could have been hauling the load of all those feelings. Maybe it was all there! Maybe the sisters' sentence bore the weight of faith, anger, regret, disappointment, and hope, because maybe all of that was churning in their hearts and written on their faces.

Of all the things that could be said about the sisters, that makes most sense to me. After all, when was the last time you felt only one single emotion? It is a rare moment in life when we feel utterly unmixed anything. There are, of course, some occasions of unmixed grief and untarnished joy and unscarred faith. But tell the truth: they are few, and they are far between. The stream of life in which we wade usually flows with more than one current of emotion.

We feel sadness at the funeral, but we feel relief that his suffering is over. We don't know how they will make it, but we manage to feel the joy of the wedding alongside our fear for the marriage. We are devastated by the physician's diagnosis, but we are hopeful about the possible treatments. We are reprimanding our toddler for acting out, but on the inside we are laughing because she really was funny. We are proud of our teenager who is becoming quite a full-grown person, and we are worried sick over the prospect of letting her go. We are sad to see the relationship end, but we are glad that things are resolved. At our daughter's graduation and at our husband's retirement we learned the rather neat trick of weeping a tear of joy in our left eye and wiping a tear of sadness from our right eye. The stream of life in which we wade usually flows with more than one current of emotion.

I rather suspect that the sisters' sentence carried the weight of faith, anger, regret, disappointment, hope, and who knows what all else. After all, their brother was dead. Someone whom they loved more than life itself was gone. Life was changing on them. The center had moved. Things were not the same. The ground of life was shifting beneath their feet. Things were not turning out the way they had planned. And, frankly, they had felt the absence of Jesus in their moment of loss. Now that they were in his presence, they brought up the fact that he had been conspicuous by his absence. And yet they hinted at hope: "If you had been here, our brother would not have died, but even now, even now, maybe . . . " The sisters' sentence says a lot. It says a lot about them, and it says a lot about you and me.

We look an awful lot like the sisters today. We have experienced what they experienced. We have felt what they felt. We have either said what they said or we have wanted to and did not do it. We have felt the hard blows of the twists and turns of life. We have stood by the open grave. We have sponged at the raging fever. We have sat by the all-night bed. We have waited on the all-day surgery. We have heard our parents breath to the rhythmic beeps and blinks of intensive care artillery. We have been stunned by the biopsy. We have been stung by the criticism.

We have stood with the sisters where the ground shifts beneath our feet and life turns out differently from the way we had it planned. And we have turned those twins into triplets. We have made their duet into a trio. We have given our own echo to their shared ditto. "Lord, I wish you had intervened. I wish you had kept this from happening. But even now, maybe, you can make something good out of all this pain." We look like the sisters, what with our faces full of faith, anger, regret, disappointment, and hope.

Hope is the last word. Hope was the last word then; hope is the last word now. Jesus hurt with Mary and Martha. Jesus walked with Mary and Martha. Jesus wept with Mary and Martha. And then, despite the fact that the sisters' faith was all mingled in with anger, regret, and disappointment, Jesus gave the sisters more than they hoped. Jesus raised Lazarus from his grave to live a little while longer.

And then, a little while later, God raised Jesus from his grave to live forever. This is the ground of our hope. The resurrection tells us that this is God's world. The resurrection tells us that, while the worst things can and do happen, the worst thing that happens is never, never, never the last thing that happens.[1] The resurrection is our last and only reason to whisper hope.

Hope is not the only word we know. We know other words, words like anger, regret, disappointment, absence, death, sorrow, and loss. Hope is not the only word. Hope is just the last word. Those other words, frankly, are not put to flight by hope. Those other words are not erased or silenced by hope, but they do change colors in the light of hope. Their dreadful darkness is altered by the Easter-colored light of hope. Those other words are embarrassed by the power of the last word. They are outlasted by the enduring, unexhausted, last word of life. This is God's world. In God's world, the worst word said is never the last word heard. In God's world, the last word standing will be hope. Mary and Martha felt a lot of different emotions when life turned hard and things went wrong, but in the presence of Christ the last thing they felt was hope.

Those sisters. Are they not a sight, weeping tears, whispering hope, and waiting for a resurrection they do not even know is coming? Those sisters. They look just alike, don't they? Those sisters look a lot like you and me. The sisters stand with us where the center moves and the ground of life shifts beneath our feet. The sisters wade with us in a stream of life that most always flows with more than one current of emotion. And finally, the sisters stumble with us in the direction of resurrection: weeping tears, feeling pain, and whispering hope. Hope was the last thing they felt. Hope will be the last word spoken. When all is said, and all is done, the last thing done will be God's, and the last word said will be hope. Amen.

Notes

[1]The phrase, "The worst thing is never the last thing," is attributed to Frederick Buechner (source unknown).